What Adults Don't Know About Art

Published in 2020 by The School of Life
First published in the USA in 2021
70 Marchmont Street, London WC1N 1AB

Copyright © The School of Life 2020
Design and illustrations by Studio Katie Kerr

Printed in Latvia by Livonia

All rights reserved. This book is sold subject to the condition that it shall not be resold, lent, hired out or otherwise circulated without express prior consent of the publisher. Every effort has been made to contact the copyright holders of the material reproduced in this book. If any have been inadvertently overlooked, the publisher will be pleased to make restitution at the earliest opportunity.

The School of Life offers programmes, publications and services to assist modern individuals in their quest to live more engaged and meaningful lives. We've also developed a collection of content-rich, design-led retail products to promote useful insights and ideas from culture.

www.theschooloflife.com

ISBN 978-1-912891-29-0

10 9 8 7 6 5 4 3 2

What Adults Don't Know About Art

Inspiring young minds to love and enjoy art

THE SCHOOL OF LIFE PRESS

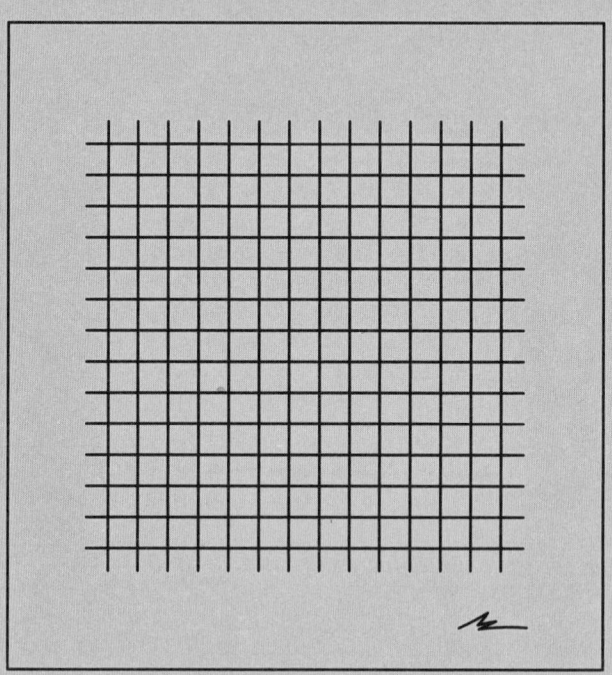

Contents

You and Art   1

The Big Question No One Answers   8

Why an Art Gallery is like Your Bedroom   16

The Big Answer   29

Why Art Galleries are Boring   32

Why a Work of Art is like a Tool   38

    Remembering   42
    Appreciation   58
    Hope   78
    Sadness   90
    Balance   100
    Making sense of money   114

Conclusion   128

You and Art

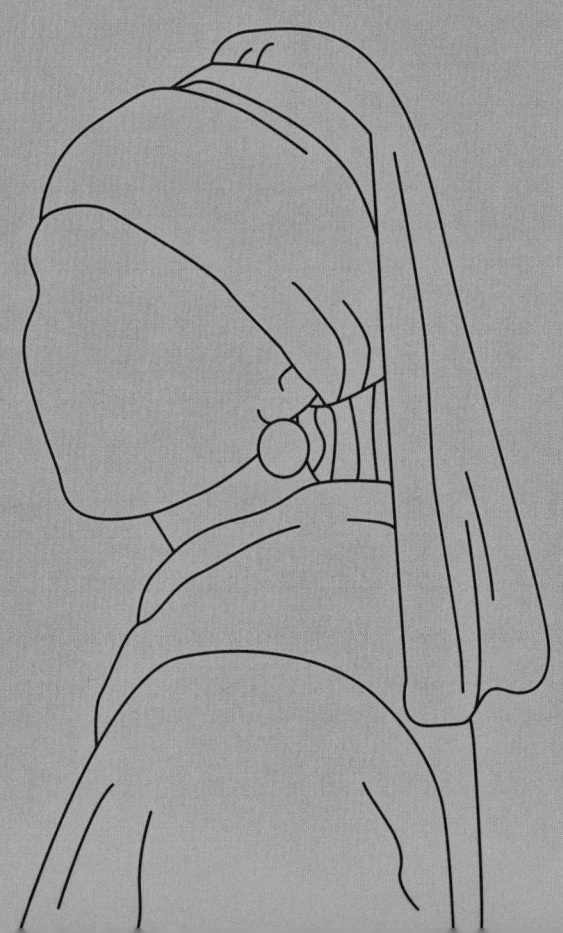

You might not know it, but you have probably been interested in art for a long time.

Perhaps it began one afternoon when you were in the kitchen. You got some coloured pens and a big sheet of paper and you drew something like this:

Drawing by Stacey, aged 6

You really enjoyed colouring the clouds blue and you were pleased with the yellow house. Dad stuck it up on the fridge door. He said he liked his hairstyle in the picture.

Or maybe the first art you really liked was a picture in a book, like this one:

Judith Kerr, *The Tiger Who Came to Tea*, 1968

You thought it would be fun to be there with a big friendly tiger drinking from a teapot.

Probably no one told you these were art.

That is a pity, because they are art — and they are fun, interesting and important to you. Instead, when you first heard about art it was probably about things that seemed very different to these: more complicated and not really connected to you.

Maybe you went to a museum or gallery when you were on holiday or on a school trip.

A visit to an art gallery

The museum was huge and there were lots of people — you kept worrying someone was going to bump into you. Nobody said very much and when they talked they spoke quietly, as if this was a very special place where you had to be on your best behaviour. You were told you weren't allowed to run about or make a noise.

There might have been lots of different pictures on the walls that you couldn't make much sense of.

Maybe you saw one like this:

Andrea del Sarto, *Madonna of the Harpies*, 1517

Looking at this picture, you might wonder why that little boy's mum is standing on a carved stone, or why the children with wings are holding her legs. Is she going to fall off?

Or perhaps you saw something a bit like this:

Constantin Brancusi, *Fish*, 1926

It sort of looks like a table... but don't try putting a glass of orange juice on it or else an alarm will ring and the guards will be very angry!

Though it looks like furniture, this is art, too. A lot of art is pictures and paintings, but there are plenty of other kinds of art too, like sculpture and textiles and installation.

Most of the time, though, when you were in the museum, you just saw the backs of people who were standing in the way.

Leonardo da Vinci, Mona Lisa, c.1503–1519
At the Louvre, Paris

Grown-ups want you to go to art galleries and museums — even if they do not go to them very often themselves. They like it if your school organises a trip to a museum.

The Big Question
No One Answers

(Until Now)

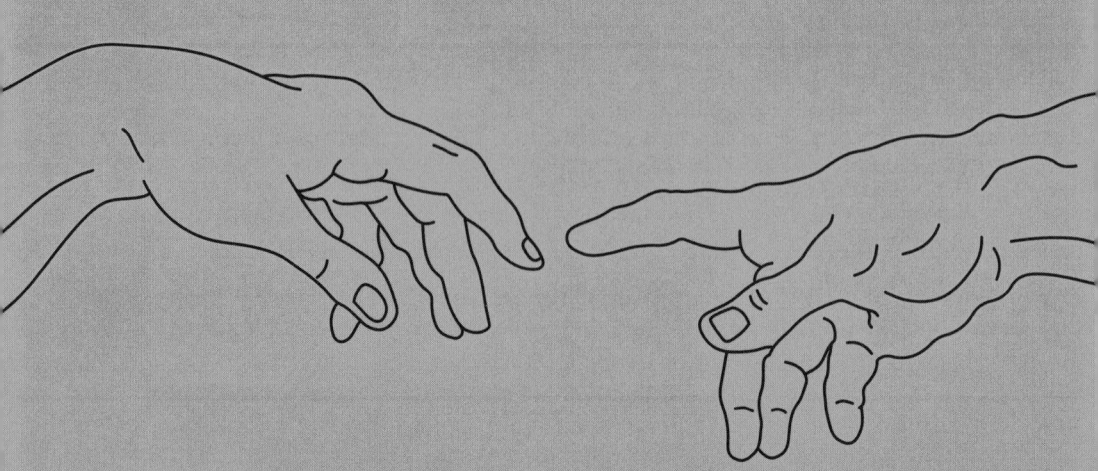

If you ask a grown-up, 'Is art important?' they'll probably say:

Yes, it's very important.

But suppose you ask a *big* question. Suppose you ask:

Why is it important?

What might an adult say if you ask this question? Perhaps they might say:

Because it's very old.

But this is not a very good answer, because a stone is very old too — actually much, much older than any work of art — and they don't ask you to go and admire a pebble. They might say:

Because it looks so real.

But that is not a great answer either. All the photos on your phone look real too, and they're always telling you to get off your phone. And anyway, lots of art doesn't look very real at all. Or they could say:

Because it costs a lot.

But that's not convincing at all: the most expensive art in the world costs about the same as an oil tanker and most art costs much less than that. But grown-ups don't go around saying how wonderful oil tankers are or have special places in the middle of big cities where you can go and look at them, and they never worry that your school doesn't spend enough time teaching you about container vessels.

Parc de Montjuïc, Barcelona, Spain

In short, if you really ask a grown-up *why* art is important, they probably wouldn't be able to give you a very good answer.*

But maybe it's not very fair to expect all grown-ups to know why art is important. There are lots of things the grown-ups you know don't understand, but that doesn't mean there is not a good answer. They don't know (really) how their phone works, but someone, somewhere, knows perfectly well.

* An adult might be surprised if you ask this because hardly any one does ask this question, even though it's a pretty obvious thing to ask, once you think about it.

So perhaps, instead, the answer could be in a book about art. There are lots of books about art, so surely one of them must cover it. But actually, most art books do not tell you why art matters. They tell you: *what the famous pictures are*.

But this isn't a huge help. Just because something is famous doesn't mean you should be interested in it. It would be a bit of a surprise if the grown-ups said:

We have to take some trips to visit famous airports! We'll start with Heathrow and then maybe go and see Schiphol, it's one of the most famous airports in Europe.

Or imagine if your mum said:

I want to go to Chile so I can see the Escondida copper mine, it's the most famous copper mine in the world!

Escondida copper mine, Chile

If they're not talking about which pictures are famous, books about art usually tell you: who the great artists are. They will probably mention some of these people:

PICASSO   FRIDA KAHLO   ANDY WARHOL

CLAUDE MONET   GEORGIA O'KEEFFE   YAYOI KUSAMA

But going through names is not actually a very convincing answer to the question of why we should care about art. You could find a book to tell you who the great dentists and great dog trainers in the world are.

Or you could make a list of the people who have had the greatest influence in the development of fridges and freezers:

WILLIAM CULLEN   CARL VON LINDE   BEULAH LOUISE HENRY

Usually your school and parents are not trying to get you interested in fridge and freezer people. Of course, it's really great that these people helped us keep our vegetables fresh, but we don't need to spend a lot of time finding out about them. You could be completely fine if you never heard another word about them in your life.

So, even though we have asked adults and looked in books about art, we still haven't got an answer to the *big* question:

Why is art important?

Books and people say art is important, but they don't say why. This can feel really odd: You're used to the idea that the adult world understands everything, even if no one gets around to explaining everything to you. But sometimes if you really push for an answer you realise that no one has an obvious one to give you.

But maybe it is not so strange really — there are plenty of important questions adults haven't got good answers to yet. For instance:

How can you make a big city beautiful?

No one really knows the answer to this — which is why there are not any really big cities where all the different districts are lovely. Or:

What's the best way to organise a school?

Perhaps hardly anyone knows because there are very few really brilliant schools. It's not that there can't be good answers to these questions. It's just that adults have not found the answers *yet*. So maybe it's the same with art. It's not that there can't be a good answer to the *big* question, it's just that we haven't found the answer yet. In this book we're going to be doing something new and unusual: We're going to find an answer to a big question…

Why might some works of art be important to you?

It's a bit like being an explorer. There were the first people to go to the North Pole, then the first people to climb to the top of Mount Everest, then the first people to go to the moon.

Robert McCall, The Space Mural, A Cosmic View, 1976
Smithsonian National Air and Space Museum, Washington, USA

The same thing can happen for questions and ideas. We are going to explore this big question, for the first time, together in this book. We are adventurers in big ideas.

15

Why an Art Gallery is like Your Bedroom

We have talked about big art galleries with lots of people and lots of paintings hung on the walls in ornate frames.

National Gallery Victoria, Melbourne, Australia

But to understand why art is important to you, we need to think about a place that sounds like the complete opposite of an art gallery:

Think about your ideal bedroom.

Imagine you've got a new bedroom and you can put anything on the walls. It's just for you — no one is going to complain or say you can't do something or that anything is silly. It's your space. It's totally up to you. What would you put up?

Maybe some things like these:

You put up posters because you like looking at them and they show things that mean a lot to you. Your room is an exciting and important place: all around you are lots of reminders of the things you love. It might be, for you, the nicest room in the world.

You might think your room is very different from a museum*:

The Tribuna in the Uffizi gallery, Florence, Italy

Compare this to your room. You have just got some posters stuck up with pins or Blu-Tack, and the gallery has pictures that are hundreds of years old in golden frames. Your room has a bed in it, but this place has marble statues instead — and there's definitely nowhere to hang your clothes.

But in an important way your ideal room and the gallery are the *same*.

---

* Normally this gallery is packed with silent adults. It's got a strange name, the Uffizi, which means 'the offices' because a long time ago it was built above the offices of a bank. You have to queue for hours just to get in. It's in a city in Italy called Florence. People travel from all round the world just to visit.

Works of art are really just special posters that other people have wanted to put in their rooms. And your room is really a private version of a gallery.

This isn't so odd: Some galleries actually started out as other people's special rooms.*

Sir John Soane's Museum, Lincoln's Inn Fields, London

* The person who lived here liked having breakfast in this room. But you can't eat a slice of toast in it these days because it's been turned into an art gallery.

In 1813, an architect called John Soane reorganised this room, in his home in London. It was his favourite room in the house. He hung all his favourite paintings and drawings on the walls and he put his favourite books in the bookcase. There are interesting shells he collected in the room, too, because he liked their shapes and colours, and there are models of buildings he liked.

It would be funny if he could come back to life (he died in 1837) and see people visiting his special room. They'd be quietly admiring the works of art and he'd be thinking:

That's where I left that book, I've been looking for it for about two hundred years!

Or he'd see a small stain on the carpet and remember that one morning a friend of his knocked over a cup of tea.

For him, everything in the room would have a very personal meaning: a little drawing of a place he liked to go on holiday, or of somewhere he wanted to go but never got the chance to visit (Soane dreamt of going to Egypt but it was extremely difficult to travel there while he was alive); some books with illustrations in them that he loved looking at; a special fossil he picked up while out for a walk.

Even if an art gallery did not actually begin as someone's house, a lot of the art on the walls really did start out as things people had in their own rooms.

This picture was a special poster for the King's bedroom*:

Anthony Van Dyck, Charles I (1600-1649) with M. de St Antoine, 1633

Because he was a king he didn't buy a poster in a shop, he got a famous artist to make one especially for him — and he needed a huge room too, because the picture is about 3.5 metres high.

* The man on the horse is King Charles I of England. The picture was painted by his friend, Anthony van Dyck, in 1633. Sometimes the King rode his horse right into his palace. He was the King, so no one could say 'Charles, I've told you before, don't ride your horse in the house, you'll get mud all over the carpet!'

22

In the same way as King Charles had an enormous and very expensive poster of himself in his room, other people might have had special posters of their relatives hung in their rooms — just like your gran might like to have a picture of you when you were little in her room (or maybe just in the living room).*

Titian, Clarissa Strozzi (1540-1581), 1542

* This little girl was called Clarissa. Her parents had to move far away, so they had this picture painted so that Clarissa's aunts and uncles could see what she looked like. It was painted nearly five hundred years ago by the most famous artist in the world at that time, a man called Titian.

Or maybe, instead of admiring musicians or tennis stars and having posters of them on their walls, someone might have been really interested in ancient Greek and Roman stories (in the past these were people's favourite stories). In this case, they would ask someone to paint them a picture of the most exciting bit in the story.*

JMW Turner, *Ulysses deriding Polyphemus*, 1829

* In the past, some of the most loved stories in the world were about a man called Ulysses. This picture is about when Ulysses and his friends land on an island. It seems great, but it's actually inhabited by giants. One of them captures them and keeps them in his cave. They think they've had it, but Ulysses comes up with a clever plan. The giant has sheep that sleep in the cave. When he lets them out in the morning, Ulysses and his friends hide amongst the flock. They run back to their boat, but the giant realises they've escaped. He throws rocks at them as they row away (you can just about see the giant's head and shoulders emerging behind the hill) but they miss the ship. The giant shouts out to Ulysses: 'What's your name?' And Ulysses, thinking fast, shouts in reply 'I'm nobody.' The giant is pretty stupid and calls out to the other giants 'Help! Nobody is escaping!' Of course the other giants don't come to help — since nobody is escaping. Ulysses and his friends are safe and they head off to their next exciting adventure.

People made their own posters, too. This one is by Vincent van Gogh, a famous painter who lived in the 19th century. It's a picture of one of his friends, Eugène Boch.*

Vincent van Gogh, Portrait of Eugène Boch, 1888

* Eugène's family owned a factory and they were very wealthy. His sister, Anna, was a painter, and they got on well. He was friends with lots of artists, and he used to help them if they were short of money (which they often were). One of his best friends was the artist Vincent van Gogh, who painted this picture.

After Vincent van Gogh created this poster, he hung it in his bedroom.* And then he made another poster — of his bedroom with this poster in it! Here it is:

Vincent van Gogh, *Bedroom*, 1888

You can just about see the picture of his friend Eugène, in his yellow jacket, above the bed. It would be amazing if Vincent had hung this picture of his bedroom in his bedroom and then made another picture of that, and hung that picture in his bedroom, and then made a poster of that, and hung that poster in his bedroom and then... but we'll make our heads hurt if we think about this too much.

* This was van Gogh's bedroom when he was living in Arles in France. He liked it so much he painted several paintings of it. This is the first one he did in 1888.

In around 1660, the English artist Mary Beale wanted a picture of her son Bartholomew*, so she made one herself.

Mary Beale, Sketch of the Artist's Son, Bartholomew Beale, Facing Left, c. 1660

She made the picture because she knew that one day her son would grow up and change — he'd still be nice, but he would be different, and she wanted to remember what he looked like when he was little. It would be nice for him, too. This is because in those days, unless someone painted a picture of you when you were small (which was very rare) you'd actually never know what you had looked like.

* Bartholomew was about five when his mother painted him. They were living in London at the time, but later Mary made money from selling her paintings and the family moved to a nice house in the countryside. When he grew up Bartholomew became a doctor.

Today, all these special 'posters' are in galleries or museums where many people can see them.

Van Gogh Museum, Amsterdam, the Netherlands

But they started out just as things that other people wanted in their own rooms.

Just by being interested in decorating your bedroom, you're already connected with the people who have loved art in the past. They were selecting posters for their room, in the same way you might select posters for yours. So, there's some very important questions you can ask about any work of art:

Why did someone want to have this picture in their room?
What did they like about it, and why?
Why was it nice for them to have it around all the time?

The Big Answer

Now we're ready to answer the big question. Remember, the question is not 'What are the most famous works of art?' or, 'Who are the greatest artists?' It is a much more important question than that. It's a question about you.

The *big* question is:

Why is art important — to you?

The answer is:

A work of art is important to you *if* you'd like to have it in your ideal room.

And:

An art gallery is important to you because it contains *suggestions* about what you *might* like to have in your room.

Right now, you might not have worked out all the things it could be really great to have in your room. There might also be lots of posters and pictures you'd love — but you do not know about them yet.

All the people who have made and collected art are speaking to you. They're saying: We liked these things in our rooms. Maybe there's something here that might excite you as well.

Most of the art in the world will not excite you, and that is completely fine. You don't need to like everything, and you do not need to have a huge number of things in your room.

You just need to find the few things that are most meaningful to you.

National Gallery of Victoria, Melbourne, Australia

Finding these things is a project that you are starting right now, and that can go on for the whole of your life.

Why Art Galleries are Boring

We have been saying that art is really about your ideal room and that art galleries are like massive bedrooms. The weird thing is though that you can have a nice time thinking about what you might put in your room, but a gallery can be quite dull and frustrating.

The reason is that, sadly, art galleries have forgotten that they are really just bedrooms. Instead, they have become more like exam halls at a university.

If you're in a gallery you will usually see little notes next to the works of art. You might even notice adults looking at them very carefully, with serious expressions on their faces.

Rijksmuseum, Amsterdam, the Netherlands

Let's take this picture, for instance*:

Claude Lorrain, Landscape with David at the Cave of Adullam, 1658

Here's the label that might go beside it:

Claude Lorrain (1600-1682)
Landscape with David at the Cave of Adullam, 1658, Oil on canvas

Painted in 1658 for Prince Agostino Chigi (1634-1705), this work depicts King David with his followers outside the cave of Adullam. David longed for water from the well of Bethlehem. Three mighty men broke through the army of the Philistines to fetch the water for him. When they returned, David realised he had unnecessarily risked their lives and instead poured the water out for the Lord (2 Samuel 23: 13-17).
A number of preparatory drawings by Claude are known.

* Claude Lorrain was famous for painting hills and valleys, but he wasn't very good at painting people. The heads looked too small and the limbs weren't quite right.

Reading this label makes you feel as if you're preparing for an exam. If you are going to pass you will need to be able to answer these questions. Are you ready? You're not allowed to look at the label again — no cheating!

Q.   Who painted this picture?
A.   *Someone called Claude Lorrain.*

Well done, that was on the label. Good memory!

Q.   When was it painted?
A.   *1658.*

But that doesn't help much unless you know about other things that happened then.

Q.   What does (2 Samuel 23: 13-17) mean?
A.   *It refers to a story in the Bible.*

The label expects you to know this. But practically no one knows about this story.

Q.   Who was Agostino Chigi?
A.   *A prince.*

That's right, the label says he was a prince, but do you know anything else about him? If you asked a million adults it would be amazing if even one of them had heard of him.

Q.   Why is it important that a number of preparatory drawings by Claude are known?
A.   *Because it proves that this picture really was painted by Claude Lorrain, not by someone else.*

Were you thinking: 'Oh I really, really hope this *is* by someone called Claude and not by someone else I have never heard of?' Be honest...

Maybe it's not surprising that a lot of people are very quiet in art galleries: they're worried someone is going to ask them some very hard questions they don't know the answers to.

It is all a bit daunting and off-putting. All this seriousness and all these boring facts make you feel that you don't know anything at all. It feels like just because you don't know all the names and dates on the little labels, you've no business looking at pictures.

But there's good news here. Because actually none of this matters very much at all. Remember, you are trying to find something for *your* room — something that you love and that you want to have around you for a long time. The exam questions don't help you love the picture.

Loving a work of art is a bit like making a new friend. You become friends with someone because you like doing things with them. You like playing football with them or chatting or joking with them or going to the park together.

It'd be astonishing if people said you could not be friends with someone unless you took an exam about them first, showing you know what year their mum was born or what their dad's middle name is. You might eventually find out these things, but they are nothing at all to do with why you like your friend.

Just like how there might be one thing you really love about your friend, maybe there is just one part of the picture that particularly interests you.*

Detail from Claude Lorrain, *Landscape with David at the Cave of Adullam*, 1658

Art isn't really boring. But it can be made boring if it gets turned into an exam.

* Lorrain loved clambering up the steep sides of hills, holding on to the branches of trees. In this picture, it's great how you can see through the arch in the cliff to see the light on the rock behind. You can imagine climbing up there. Be careful you don't fall! Maybe there's a cave where you could have a picnic?

Why a Work of Art is like a Tool

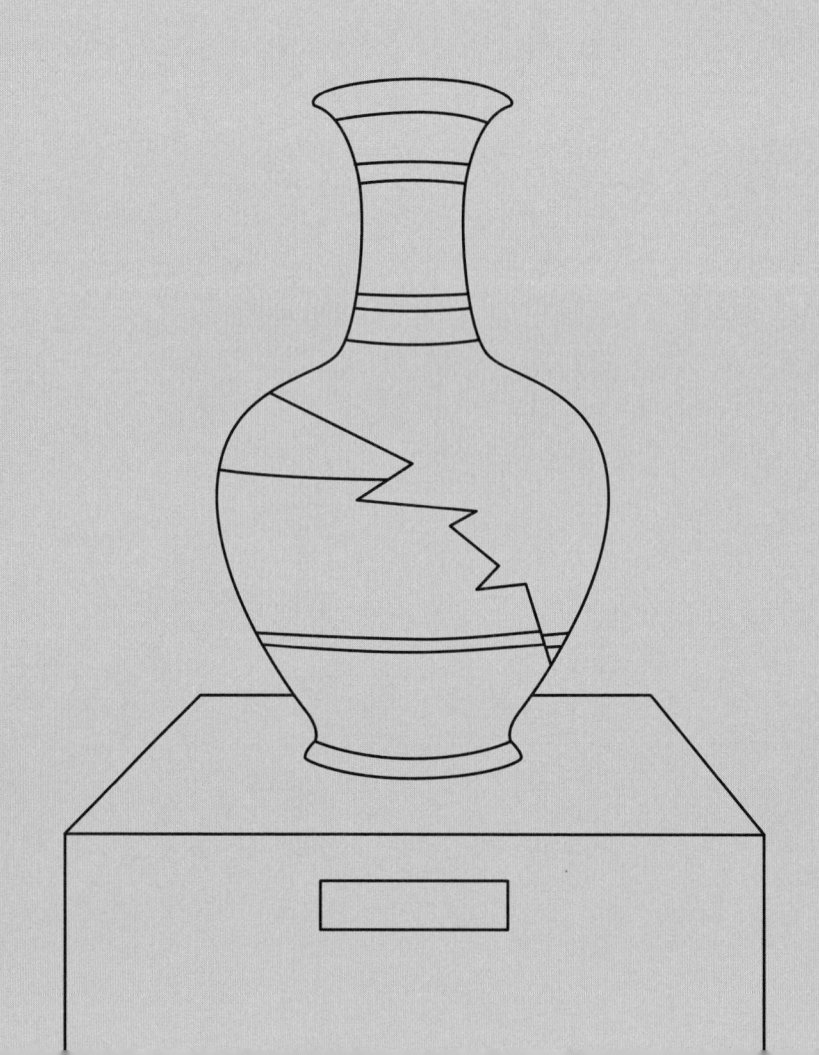

In the previous chapters we have discussed how the idea of choosing posters to decorate your ideal room is a very helpful way to understand art and why it's important.

But there's one more big idea that's also very helpful for this, and it might be unexpected:

Works of art are tools.

Maybe that sounds pretty strange? That's because normally we think of tools as things that help our bodies to do things.

Our hands are really bad at carrying water, so people invented a tool — a bucket — to help us with the job. It is impossible to cut wood with your fingers (please do not try!), so people invented saws, which are much, much better at the task.

Jean-Francois Millet, *The Wood Sawyers*, 1850–1852

But there are other tools that do not help our bodies: they help our brains. Imagine your dad is going to the shops. He might forget what to buy because his brain isn't very good at remembering everything. He needs a special kind of brain tool: a shopping list. That way he'll be sure to get the frozen peas and the milk. (He doesn't really need to add chocolate biscuits to the list because he never forgets those…)

There are actually quite a lot of different brain tools:

CALCULATORS
Because our brains are pretty bad at working out what 113×92 is.*

CLOCKS
Because our brains aren't much good at guessing what time it is.

MAPS
Because we aren't very good at working out directions on our own.

* 10,396, in case you were wondering.

While these are all important, some of the most interesting and useful brain tools are actually works of art.

Remembering	Appreciation
Hope	Sadness
Balance	Making sense of money

Maybe it doesn't feel obvious just yet how art can be a tool for these things, or why you need these tools, or even what 'appreciation' and 'balance' mean and have to do with you. In the next chapters we'll explain them. Let's get started!

Remembering

You have got a bad memory. That's not a mean thing to say because everyone has a bad memory, and we all have bad memories in the same, important way.

It's not that you forget your name and address or what 8 + 7 is... hopefully! But there are other memories that quite easily slip away. Probably you remember some things about your sixth birthday, but lots of details get lost. Maybe, at one point during the day, your dad smiled at you in a really special way — he was thinking of the day, exactly six years ago, when you were born.

John Singer Sargent, *The Birthday Party*, 1887

He hardly ever smiles in exactly that way. It would be a lovely thing to have in your memory, but it has disappeared.

Or, maybe there was a moment when you were opening an exciting present and your little sister was happy because you were happy. It would be good to remember that moment, because sometimes sisters can be quite annoying and that moment would remind you how much your happiness means to her. But, sadly, the memory has gone.

Your mind is like a big messy cupboard.

There are lots and lots of interesting things in there but some of them are right at the back, so when you open the cupboard door you don't see them: you just see the things at the front.

It's similar with memories. There are lots of memories in your 'mind-cupboard', but a lot of them get hidden away in the corners at the back, so you hardly even realise they are there. But if you could access those lost memories, they could be wonderful and really useful.

What a work of art can do is help you to keep memories at the front of your mind where you can get at them easily and quickly.

Art is a tool for remembering.

Here's a story about how art began.

Art has been around for a very, very long time and nobody really knows how it started. One of the main ideas is that people make art because they want to remember things.

The story goes like this:

> Long ago, in ancient Greece, there was a boy who was a shepherd. He was good friends with a girl who lived in the same village. During the winter and spring they could see each other practically every day, go for walks and have long chats together.
>
> But then the summer came round. That was a very big problem. In those days, in summer, shepherds would have to take their sheep far away, up to the mountains to feed on the new grass. This meant that the shepherd boy and his friend wouldn't see each other for months.
>
> On the last day before the boy had to leave, he was sitting together with the girl feeling sad, and the girl noticed his shadow on the wall. She got a soft bit of stone and started tracing the outline of his shadow. She made a picture of him so she wouldn't forget him — and his nice hair and nose — while he was away.

Jean Baptiste Regnault, *The Origin of Painting: Dibutades Tracing the Portrait of a Shepherd*, 1785

This was the first time people realised something important:

A picture helps you to remember.

It is why your granny likes to have photos of you. There's a lot of things that you might try to remember. Some artists are interested in making memory-pictures of special moments in their children's lives.

One evening, a very long time ago back in 1756, Thomas Gainsborough's two young daughters were in the garden. It was getting late and they'd been told they had to go back indoors. Then the little one saw a white butterfly beside them. She was filled with wonder at this beautiful, strange creature, fluttering right past her and she wanted to hold it, but her big sister said they had to go in (even though she was quite interested in the butterfly as well). It was a lovely moment.*

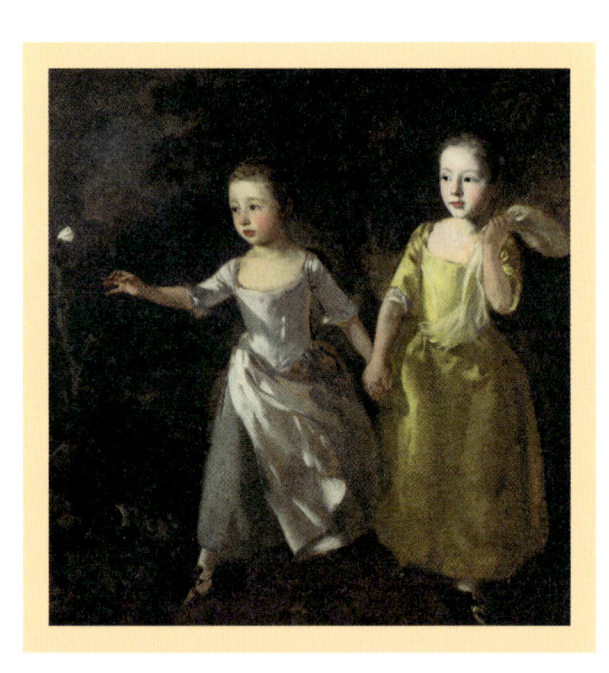

Thomas Gainsborough, The Painter's Daughters Chasing a Butterfly, c. 1756

Gainsborough decided to paint a picture so that he'd always remember that moment. When you're 6 or 7 you think you'll stay like that forever, but he knew his daughters would grow up, and they might not remember this special moment. Just like a butterfly, the memory is there for a moment, then you never see it again.

* Gainsborough was one of the most successful portrait painters in 18th century England. He specialised in painting pictures of wealthy people looking elegant and serious (which they weren't always in real life). Sometimes, to please himself, he also painted pictures of his family, like this one of his daughters.

Imagine what it would have been like for the little girls, when they were older, to look back at this picture. In those days, photographs hadn't been invented yet, and hardly anyone ever got to see a picture of themselves when they were young.

If you could ask an artist to help you remember some special moments in your life, what might they be? Don't worry if you can't think of any straight away — maybe you'll think of your answer tomorrow, or next week or even next year.

It's not just special moments with people that you might want to remember, though. You might want to remember a place. Somewhere interesting you went on holiday, or even a really amazing view.

Imagine that you went on a holiday to Japan (a lot of thinking involves imagining things!) You might go on a super fast train and see Mount Fuji.

A bullet train by Mount Fuji, Japan

That would be great. But for you, that might not be the most important thing that happens. Instead, it might be that one day there was a lot of mist, and it looked really beautiful.

More than four hundred years ago, there lived a Japanese artist called Hasegawa Tōhaku. He loved misty days too. He liked how you could look into the forest, and just see a few of the trees through the thick white air — if you took two steps back some of the trees would completely disappear, and if you took two steps forward you would see some more start to emerge.

Tōhaku made a picture to help him remember what it was like (because usually it wasn't misty).*

Hasegawa Tōhaku, Pine Trees / left hand screen, 16th century

---

* You might imagine art as things in frames that you hang on a wall. But in Japan, a lot of art was painted on tall folding screens as high as a person. Each of the vertical lines in the picture is actually a joint. The screens could be folded so that they could stand up on their own and moved around a room.

One painter in history really liked muddy fields, especially in the evening. On one particular day it had been raining non-stop, and then the sun came out. There was a lovely sunset. He decided to go out for a walk, and while he was out he saw a muddy field. Looking at the field, he felt small and the world seemed very big, but in a lovely way. He didn't want to forget that place or that feeling, so he painted this picture*:

Caspar David Friedrich, The Grosse Gehege near Dresden, c. 1832

The mist or a puddle might not be exactly what you want to remember. But hopefully they give you some suggestions about things that could be important to you. What's *your* version of a muddy puddle or seeing a tree through the mist? What do you like to look at, and remember?

* Caspar David Friedrich lived in Germany in the 19th century. He loved taking long walks alone in the countryside. His favourite times of day were dawn and dusk. Friedrich felt that nature was speaking to him about his life.

Sometimes the memory that you want to hold onto is not a person or a place, it's the way you *feel*.

That's what this next picture is doing: It's preserving a mood or a feeling.*

Hilaire-Germain-Edgar Degas, Beach Scene, c. 1869–1870

In this picture, the other children have gone swimming, but the girl under the umbrella is feeling more dreamy. She does not feel like changing into her swimming costume (that's the brown suit laid out on the right, which is what swimsuits looked like in those days). Instead, she wants to lie on the sand, look up at the sky and wonder about things.

* This picture was painted by Hilaire-Germain-Edgar Degas. Degas was born in France in 1834. His family was quite rich and his father wanted him to become a lawyer or a banker, but he chose to be an artist instead. He lived in America for a few years, then he moved to Paris. He often went on holiday to the seaside.

You can imagine that she was having interesting thoughts:

I don't want to go swimming…
Maybe I don't quite know what I want to do…
How do people find out what to do?
What might my life be like when I am grown-up?
Once I was a baby, but I'm not anymore…
How will I change in the future?
What's it like being a grown-up?

Perhaps you sometimes feel like this, too. It's an important mood: Your mind is starting to explore some big, difficult, fascinating questions.

As well as by making pictures of people, places or things that capture a certain mood, there's another way artists can help you remember a feeling: They can make an 'abstract' picture.

It's called 'abstract' because it doesn't look like anything you normally see.

It's a picture of what a feeling *feels* like.

There are times when you're feeling bouncy and happy, like maybe you want to jump around a bit. That might be how the artist was feeling when they painted the picture on the next page. They put some vivid colours together to make a bright, abstract painting.

Cy Twombly, Untitled, 2000–2001

But even though you do feel ecstatic sometimes, feelings change, and you will not always be in such a jolly mood.* When you look at a picture like this it reminds you of the happy feeling you had, and maybe helps it come back.

* Cy Twombly, who painted this picture, was born in Virginia in the US in 1928. His father was a very famous baseball player. He knew he wanted to be an artist from the age of twelve. Though people said his style was new and shocking, he often got his ideas by studying very old things, like ancient Greek myths.

Art can also be used to remember an idea.

One day, a very long time ago, in the 14th century, the ruler of Japan knocked over a bowl. It fell on the floor and broke into pieces. It was a simple bowl but he liked it very much: he used to drink his favourite tea from it every day. He was very upset.

Instead of just throwing the broken pieces away and getting a new bowl, one of his assistants came up with a good idea. They'd mend the bowl in a very special way, by using gold to join the pieces back together. It was very tricky to do but in the end they managed it. The bowl looked even more beautiful than before: It was a work of art.

An example of kintsugi

The ruler was so pleased that they made up a special name for this way of mending things. They called it *kintsugi*. *Kin* means 'golden' in Japanese and *tsugi* means 'joinery', or putting things together. So *kintsugi* means 'mending with gold'.

Kintsugi represents an important idea: It suggests that things that are broken can be mended, and mended so nicely that they are even better than they were before. You can still see where it was broken, but now you don't mind.

It is not just bowls that can get broken. A friendship might get damaged — someone might say something not very nice and you feel let down and upset. Maybe you feel like throwing the broken friendship away. Or maybe sometimes you feel a bit broken yourself. Everything seems to be going wrong and you just want to give up. But the idea behind kintsugi tells us that as well as bowls, friendships and people can be mended and be better than before. Saying sorry or forgiving someone strengthens a friendship. It doesn't pretend that there hasn't been a problem. If you let someone help, you can solve your problems, and you will be stronger because you've learned to ask for help when you needed it.

Kintsugi is a tricky idea and you might forget about it: It gets hidden away at the back of the cupboard. But if you look at the bowl mended with gold, it will help you remember.

Another idea we have trouble remembering about is *luck*. There are all sorts of things we can't control, and they make a big difference to how our lives turn out. You might be quite clever, but you did not make your brain, you are just lucky you have it. Or someone might be good looking, but they didn't design their face, they were just lucky. Maybe other people haven't been so lucky, but it's not their fault. When we forget about luck we become conceited and proud, and take things for granted; when we remember about luck we're kinder to others and grateful for our own good fortune. This picture helps keep the idea of luck at the front of our minds*:

French School (15th century), Dame Fortune and victims falling from her wheel, from Boccaccio's 'The Fall of Princes', 1467

* This is a page from an illustrated medieval book. There was no printing back then, so every book had to be copied out and illustrated by hand, which took ages. Hardly anyone had any books at home — not even one. This book was written in the 1300s; it tells the life stories of famous people.

The big wheel lifts people up and then as it turns it brings them down again. They have not necessarily done anything very special or very bad, but their lives go well for a while then go badly, and then maybe go well again. It is helpful to remember that things come and go in life — sometimes we might be lucky, and sometimes we might not, but we can't control it. Art like this can help us to keep this thought in our minds when we are going about our daily lives.

The idea that the artwork below is helping us to remember is really important (and really easy to forget)*:

Berthe Morisot, In a Park, c. 1874

* The painter, Berthe Morisot, hasn't put in all the details — you can't really see people's faces, for instance. She wasn't being lazy. She wanted us to feel how nice it is in the countryside without being distracted by thinking about who these people are. This type of painting is called *Impressionism*.

The painting shows a lovely moment: everyone was happy, but really nothing much was going on. They were just sitting in a field near some trees. They weren't buying nice things or going to a party.

We often forget that usually it is very simple and ordinary things like this that actually make us happy.

Good ideas can help us to be kinder and wiser, but we're not very good at keeping the important ideas at the front of our mind-cupboards. That's why we actually need the right works of art around us (in our rooms) to remind us.

Your room — your gallery — is a kind of remembering machine, just for you.

When you are deciding what you want to have in your room, one of the questions you are asking yourself is: 'What do I want to remember?' And if you are visiting a gallery, or if you are looking at a book of pictures, you are asking yourself:

Are there any clues here about what it would be good for me to remember?

And:

What should I keep right at the front of my mind-cupboard?

Appreciation

Appreciation is quite a serious, grown-up word: It might not be one you use much (or at all). But it's a helpful word because when you *appreciate* something, it's the opposite of *finding it boring*.

Art can help you to appreciate people and things.

Let's start with a problem: *feeling bored*. Maybe you get bored quite a lot, practically everyone does. You look around your life and it is all so familiar, just the same old boring stuff. Why doesn't anything exciting happen?

Probably you have got all sorts of ideas about what would be exciting. Imagine if a dinosaur walked past the window… Or what if you could blast off into space in a rocket? It would be great if you had a pet penguin. Or a cute koala. But obviously nothing like this is really going to happen. Life is so dull!

Remember we've been saying that works of art are brain-tools? Well, one of the things they can do is stop your brain from getting bored. Let's look at how that can happen. Start with something that can sound very boring indeed: *grass*. There's lots of grass around. It's green. You might think grass could be just about the least interesting thing in the whole world. Well, let's look at an artist who saw grass very carefully.

In Albrecht Dürer's picture of grass, each blade is different. You could imagine being a tiny insect wandering around looking for lunch; it would be like being in a huge jungle; you could make a little house and become friends with a ladybird. You might get chased by a worm (luckily worms are very slow).*

Albrecht Dürer, *Great Piece of Turf*, 1503

* Dürer started learning to be an artist when he was a child and became famous when he was in his twenties. He was the first person in all of Europe to draw a rhinoceros — but it wasn't very accurate because he'd never actually seen one!

What Dürer is saying is:

Grass isn't really boring at all. I made this picture to show you how interesting grass can be.

But it's not just grass. Lots of things become more interesting if you use art to help you. Imagine you've got a bike. It was fun at first but it feels pretty boring now.

One day an artist called Pablo Picasso was looking at his old bike.* He was fed up with it. So he imagined it a very different way. Picasso imagined it like this:

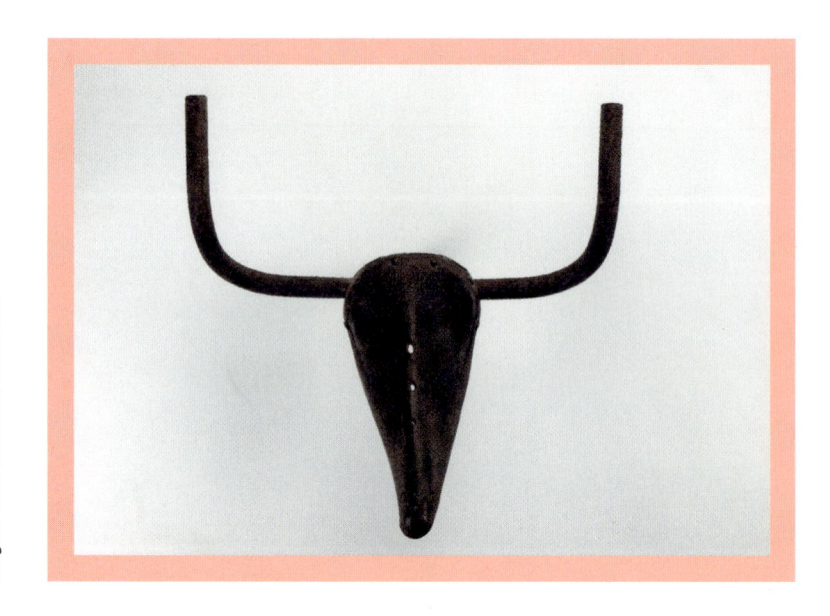

Pablo Picasso, Tête de taureau (Bull's Head), bicycle seat and handlebars, 1942

* Picasso was one of the most famous artists of the 20th century. He was born in Spain but lived a lot of his life in Paris. He was very imaginative and kept changing his styles of drawing and painting.

The next time Picasso went on his bike he imagined he was riding on the back of a bull.

So, here's a big idea. It's not really *things* that are boring. It is just that sometimes our brains don't know how to make them interesting.

We can use art as a tool to help our brains find ways of making things more exciting.

Now let's move onto another one of our big ideas around appreciation: *the importance of drawing.*

We live at a very strange point in history. For most of history, there were hardly any pictures of anything. Every picture had to be made by someone, by hand — either being drawn or painted or sculpted. Only a few people ever saw a picture of themselves.

Then, in the 1800s, photography was invented. But even after that, there weren't many pictures, because it was really complicated and expensive to take a photo. It was only for very special occasions.

Then, around the 1960s, smaller cameras were invented. They were still pretty complicated, though, with lots of switches and dials. Children weren't usually allowed even to touch them. And you couldn't see the photos until they'd been developed in a special shop. So if you'd been alive then and your mum took a photo of you playing on the beach on holiday you wouldn't get to see it until you got home.

It's only very recently (in terms of the long story of history) that it has become normal for people to have cameras in their phones. Indeed, mobile phones themselves weren't invented very long ago at all! You are among the first people ever who find it normal to see photographs of everything all the time.

That's amazing. But it's also a bit of a problem. Because when you can take lots of photos of anything you want, whenever you want, you don't actually need to look at things very carefully. Let's see how this works. Suppose you see an interesting tree. You might take a photo of it, like this one:

A tree in Serra da Arrábida, Setúbal, Portugal

That's great. Now we've got a challenge for you. On a blank piece of paper, try to do a drawing from memory of the tree. Shut this book and don't look back at the photo, just have a go. It's hard, isn't it?

When you've finished, compare your drawing to the photo. Did you notice that the tree splits about halfway up the trunk and then the left-hand part splits into three big sections, but the right-hand part splits into two main sections? Did you include the green and white moss growing up the trunk? There are bound to be lots and lots and lots of details that are different. Don't worry, it's not a test. It's just an experiment.

This experiment is telling us something important. What it's telling us is that usually we don't look very carefully at things. But when you do a drawing of something, it is the opposite. You have to look at it very carefully. Imagine you are drawing these leaves:

Some green oak leaves

You have to notice lots of details. Obviously the leaves are green, but are they all exactly the same shade? The edges are made up of little curvy bits, but each curve is different, and one is actually quite pointy. Each leaf has dark little 'veins' down the middle, but each of these is individual, too, like a fingerprint.

The first person to recognise the importance of drawing was a 19th-century English writer called John Ruskin.* This is his drawing of an old, withered leaf:

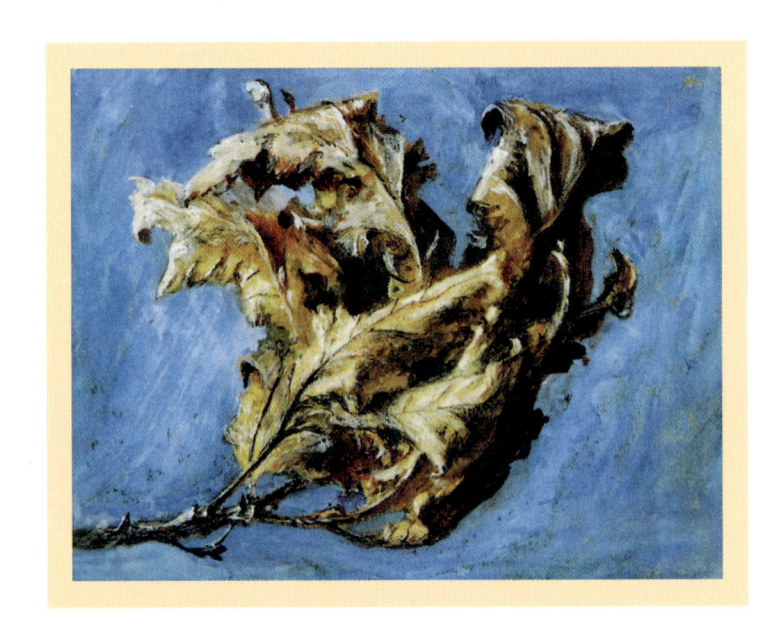

John Ruskin, Fast sketch of withered oak, 1879

* John Ruskin liked to look closely at objects in nature. When he was little he was lonely and didn't have many friends. His parents had a big garden and he loved looking carefully at the plants. In the evening his father would read to him and while he was listening John would draw pictures. Sometimes he drew imaginary pictures of castles but sometimes he'd make a drawing of whatever was around.

John Ruskin thought that everyone would be better if they spent more time drawing. He didn't think we needed to be very good at it:

The important thing is that we have to look carefully at the thing we are drawing.

When you've got your drawing brain switched on you notice much more of the world — and that makes everything more interesting. What if you did a drawing of the kitchen table or a car or someone playing football or even your own face (looking in a mirror of course)? You might realise that you'd not looked at any of these things very carefully before.

Here is another idea to consider:

Art can help us love people.

We want to love other people — our friends and family — but it's tricky because other people aren't nice all the time and lots of things can go wrong: maybe there's a disagreement or they get in a bad mood (or maybe you do).

Art can help us cope with the ups and downs of getting on with the most important people in our lives.

Looking at art can help us understand people better (even when that feels hard).

The nice thing about these Russian dolls is that the little ones are hidden inside the bigger ones. You might be looking at a big one, but you know the little ones (all the way down to the baby) are still there inside.

Russian Matryoshka dolls

It's the same with people. Mum or Dad are obviously big, but what's much less obvious is that there's a baby version of them and a 5-year-old version and a teenage version all still there inside them.

That's why adults can be so surprising. They can seem very sensible most of the time, then they panic or get upset or lose their temper. It's confusing. But maybe it's not so confusing if you think about the Russian dolls. When they get upset, it is just the baby or 5-year-old or teenage version of themselves that's bothered.

Artists have made pictures of this as well. Here's one that shows a person at every stage during their life:

D de Vosthem, Les Ages de l'homme (The Ages of Man), 16th century

They're wearing funny clothes because this engraving* was made a very long time ago, in the 16th century.

We often forget that big people used to be little, and that little people will one day be big, and eventually old. An interesting thing about loving someone is that you need to keep in mind that they weren't always the way they are now — and that they will change in the future as well.

* 'Engraving' is a way of making many copies of the same thing. First you make the drawing by cutting grooves into a metal plate. Then you put ink into the grooves. When you press a piece of paper against the plate the ink goes onto the paper to make the image. You then repeat this to make more copies.

In the 1600s there was a successful artist called Rembrandt.*
Starting in his twenties, he painted pictures of himself as he
got older. Here are a few of them:

Rembrandt, Self-Portrait, c. 1629

IN HIS TWENTIES

Rembrandt, Self-Portrait in a Flat Cap, 1642

IN HIS THIRTIES

Rembrandt, Self-Portrait, 1652

IN HIS FORTIES

Rembrandt, Self-Portrait with Two Circles, c. 1665–1669

IN HIS FIFTIES

It's very strange to see different pictures of the same person at different stages of their life all at the same time. Why is that?

Maybe you feel sorry for him. At one point he was young and strong and at another point he was successful. Then he gets old, his hair turns white, he gets wrinkles and his chin starts to sag. When he was young he didn't know how his life would go. He didn't know what successes and failures he would have. He didn't know what he would be like when he got old. But it all happened.

When we think about someone over their whole life it's easier to feel love towards them.

Everyone's life is so strange. This leads us to our next big idea:

Art helps us see what's nice about people.

Some people look pretty interesting, like movie stars and pop singers. But most of us look quite normal. If people got to know us, they would realise how fascinating and special we are — it's just that mostly we look pretty ordinary. (It's a funny thing that 'ordinary' sounds like a bad thing, but actually, of course, nearly everyone is ordinary.)

---

* Rembrandt was the most famous artist of the 17th century. He was particularly good at using shadows; he made the light fall just on a few details so you would look at them very carefully, but you can only half-see other details. He loved eating huge meals and going to parties. He was very close to his son, Titus, who became an art dealer when he grew up.

A very good thing that some artists have done is to take a seemingly ordinary-looking person and pay them a lot of loving attention.

And quite often the person they chose was their mother. Maybe you can guess why? You know your mum is very, very special — but other people looking at her might not realise it. This can be very sad.

Here's one artist who painted a picture of his mum.* If you just glanced at her you might not think she was all that nice. She looks quite grumpy and serious:

James Abbott McNeill Whistler, *Arrangement in grey and black No. 1*, 1871

In this picture, Whistler is saying: 'My mum is great!' She looks very strict. But actually she was very loving. When her son said he wanted to be an artist she helped him a lot. When he made friends that she thought were a bit odd she invited them to parties to get to know them properly — and she came to really like them too.

She's not laughing in the picture, but he knew she had a very lovely smile. Maybe she's serious not because she is boring, but because she feels such a lot of responsibility for looking after her child. She would go to a lot of trouble to make you happy, even if it was just a small thing. You don't know what she's thinking exactly, but it feels like she's thinking about taking care of you. She's not traditionally 'beautiful', but she is seen with love.

The artist is asking us to look as carefully as they looked.

They know their mother is really lovely, and they want us to see that, too. Loving someone means seeing the good things about them that aren't so obvious to other people. You could do the same with someone's dad or their granny or their little sister or their cousin. And if you can do that, it means you could do it with almost anyone.

* This was the mum of James Abbott McNeill Whistler. He was an American artist, born in 1834. He was very successful, but then he got into a terrible argument with John Ruskin (from page 64). Whistler ended up having to give almost all of his money to Ruskin. Whistler was a great artist but not very wise about money.

Sometimes it can be helpful to look at art when people aren't being so nice.

In this picture the sea looks terrible. If you were on that ship you would likely be in a huge panic — you'd think it was going to sink at any moment.*

Detail from Ludolf Bakhuysen, *Warships in a Heavy Storm*, c. 1695

---

* This picture was painted at the end of the 1600s in the Netherlands. The Netherlands had lots of very good sailors (and still does), and lots of good artists. It was the first country where ordinary people could buy paintings and they loved pictures of the things that mattered in their everyday lives — cooking, sitting with their friends, cleaning — and ships, because a lot of their businesses depended on trade with other countries.

But the point is: They're going to be fine. This ship has been in hundreds of storms before, in fact they run into a storm at some point on pretty much every voyage; the experienced sailors don't like storms, but they know they can get through them quite safely. It's the same with relationships. The picture is saying: 'It looks terrifying out there, but actually the ship is going to be fine (and you'll be fine, too).'

This might not seem like it has anything to do with love, but it does. This is because:

Art can help you with the ups and downs of the people in your life.

You see, the problem with other people is that even if they are usually lovely they are sometimes awful — just like the sea is usually calm but sometimes there is a storm and it is full of frightening waves.

When people are annoying or boring or upset or annoyed, we might panic and think, 'This person is a monster!' We feel like we might stop loving them.

But what this picture is telling us is that actually, we can cope. It might be tricky for a while, but it's not really a disaster. Your mum or your dad or friend will calm down soon, they will say they are sorry and they'll be in a good mood again. And you will go on loving them.

This is a picture that the artist Angelica Kauffman* painted of herself (in a white dress) with her friend Charlotte, who liked writing poetry. Charlotte didn't really walk around with leaves in her hair — Angelica just put them in for fun. The picture is about why two people are friends. They're different, but they help each other. Angelica is more confident and outgoing, but she's listening carefully to what Charlotte is saying. Often it was Charlotte who suggested ideas for paintings and then Angelica would go into her studio and paint them.

Angelica Kauffmann, *Artist in the Character of Design, Listening to the Inspiration of Poetry*, 1782

* Kauffman was a very successful artist. She was born in Switzerland but moved to London and Rome because there were opportunities for selling her paintings there. She had interesting friends — and liked painting pictures of them.

A friend doesn't need to be the same as you — they can be a good friend because they're better than you at some things. Instead of being envious of them, you can get your friend to help you with things you aren't as good at. That is a big idea:

Remember to appreciate your friendships, and love your friends as best you can.

Art can also remind us about the places we live in, and what they are really like. When people want to say what's nice about the place where they live, they usually talk about the things that are obviously attractive. Suppose you lived in Holland, you might show someone a picture like this and say:

This is what's great about living here:

A sightseeing boat in Holland

It is rather lovely. The problem is, it's hardly ever like this. In this picture, it's a sunny day, but actually there aren't that many sunny days in Holland. There's a nice little boat going past, but mostly the boats on the rivers are quite different — they're usually carrying coal or scrap iron. And in the picture the windmill looks like people take a lot of care of it, but they're often neglected. If you went to Holland expecting it to be just like this, you'd probably be disappointed.

Some artists think differently. Instead of showing the very nicest things about a place, they concentrate on showing how a place can be lovely in ways you wouldn't usually expect:

Jacob van Ruisdael, *The Windmill at Wijk bij Duurstede*, c. 1668–1670

It's not a very nice day; the banks of the river are messy and neglected and there's no nice boat to take you on a trip.

But the artist, Jacob van Ruisdael*, still really loves this place. He likes seeing the shadows of the clouds on the water, he likes feeling cosy inside while it is grey and cold outside, and the interesting old wooden posts that prop up the bank. He likes the weeds, and how a ray of sunlight is striking the side of the windmill, and he likes the shapes of the clouds, too. Once they are pointed out; you might like these things too.

There's a big point being made here. Often we get disappointed because we're looking for the obviously nice things, while actually there might be a lot of good things around, we just don't know how to see them.

A useful thing art can do is teach us to look in unexpected places for what we might like.

The secret of appreciation is seeing the nice things about a place or a person that aren't immediately obvious. It's how we want other people to see us, and it's how — ideally — we should see them.

---

* Van Ruisdael was born in Haarlem, Holland, in 1629. His father, uncles and brothers were all painters. In those days, being a painter was a family business. It was a skill you could learn, like being a plumber or a dentist. Nobody asked if you had a talent or if it was right for you, they just thought it was a job like any other. Jacob liked painting clouds and water so would often put the horizon low down in the picture (in this one about two-thirds of the painting is just the sky).

Hope

Sometimes it's hard to stay cheerful. It's not that anything awful or very sad has happened, we just feel glum.

Imagine that the weather has been cold and wet for ages and you've got lots of work to do for school, or maybe your best friend is away on holiday and you're stuck at home. It's not surprising if you feel pretty gloomy.

This is one of the times when you need art — because quite a lot of art has been made specifically to cheer people up.

Art is a tool for storing hopeful feelings and giving them back when we're feeling low.

One of the ways that artists do this is by painting sunny pictures that make us feel better.

The man in this painting was a wonderful architect called Karl Friedrich Schinkel, and he lived and worked in Berlin, in Germany. In Berlin, the winter lasts for months and months and the sky is usually grey. Often it was freezing and Schinkel had to wear a huge, heavy coat. It was dark when he went to work and dark when he came home. He was very busy and he hardly ever got a break to go somewhere warm on holiday.*

Franz Ludwig Catel, Schinkel in Naples, 1824

* Franz Ludwig Catel painted this picture in the early 19th century. It shows something that today feels ordinary, but in those days was still unusual: someone on holiday. There weren't any cars, trains, or planes so people just stayed at home. But a few people did travel for pleasure and often they came to a city in Italy called Naples. People liked going there because it was warm and got lots of sunshine. In the distance you can see the island of Capri, which was where, in ancient times, Roman emperors took their holidays.

But one time he did. He stayed in sunny Naples where he could open the windows and look out across the trees to the sparkling water. There was a lovely island in the distance (you could take a boat there), the sky was blue and in the evening he could have dinner outside and look up at the stars. He asked a friend to paint a picture of this so he could take it home with him. He put it on the wall of his room back in cold, dark Berlin, and every time he looked at it, it cheered him up.

Art can bottle happiness.

We don't think about it much these days, but in the past 'bottling' was a hugely important human discovery. It's a way of preserving fruits and vegetables. You used to only get strawberries for a few weeks of the year, when they were ripe in the local fields and gardens — there was no way of keeping them fresh. You couldn't transport them from another country — it would have taken weeks on ships and they'd rot. They couldn't be grown in greenhouses either, because they didn't know how to make big, clear panes of glass yet. It was a pity because a lot of people loved the taste of strawberries.

But then someone found out how to preserve strawberries. They cooked them and stored them in a jar or a bottle with a tight lid. And then they could open the jars in the middle of winter and have a taste of strawberries. It cheered them up.

Art does the same. It 'bottles' happy times; preserving them so we can have access to them when things aren't as nice.

These two paintings are called 'Renaissance' paintings:

Paolo Uccello, *The Battle of San Romano*, c. 1435–1440

Detail from: Painter of central Italy (formerly Attributed to Luciano Laurana, c. 1420–1479), *View of an Ideal City*, or *The City of God*, c. 1470

The Renaissance was an important change in thinking that happened in Italy and then across Europe from about 1400.

Renaissance means 'rebirth' in Old French — and it was called this because the people involved felt like they were rediscovering a lot of very old ideas that came from the Greeks and Romans, which were much better than the ideas that were generally around at the time. They thought you made progress not by throwing away what had gone before, but by learning from the best ideas of the past.

In the 1400s when these pictures were painted there were lots of battles in Europe. It was horrible. There would be a lot of shouting and fighting, everyone would be in a panic and it would all be very chaotic and frightening. So, during this time they liked to bottle the special times when everything was calm and peaceful — like early morning in a lovely city when there's no one around.

Another thing about the past was that it was not very easy for people to spend time alone. You can see what it might have been like in the painting, *Gossip in the Salon* above on the next page. You'd always be surrounded by people who were watching you or gossiping about you or asking you to do things or telling you long, boring stories about how their cousin's neighbour twisted their ankle. Unless you were quite rich, it was unusual to have a room of your own — like the woman in the painting on the right.*

---

* Georg Friedrich Kersting lived in Germany in the 19th century. He belonged to a movement in art called 'Biedermeier'. Biedermeier artists liked painting scenes of home life, and they loved quiet moments and tidy rooms. They were excited by questions like: How does ordinary life go well? What makes people happy?

Carl Schweninger the Younger, Gossip in the Salon, c. 1903

Detail from: Georg Friedrich Kersting, Embroidery woman, 1817

So you can understand how nice it must have been to be alone to concentrate on what you want to do; to get on with your projects and interests and to have your mind to yourself. This picture bottled a rare, lovely moment of being alone. There is nothing you have to do — but you're not bored. There's so much you want to do on your own and there's plenty of time.

It's the people in the picture's day off. They're having a party with their friends down by the river:

Pierre-Auguste Renoir, Luncheon of the Boating Party, 1880–1881

* Pierre-Auguste Renoir was an Impressionist. That means he tried to capture the feeling of a moment. An odd thing about being human is that all our experiences only last a few seconds while they are actually happening. We look up and see people sitting around the table, a moment later they've all changed positions. But some moments are really lovely and the Impressionists tried to capture with paint the happiest minutes of life.

Everyone is happy and the little dog is being sweet. Maybe they'll go swimming later or start dancing.

The artist* made this picture to bottle this cheerful day. Tomorrow they'll all be at work, wearing their work clothes, and they will have to go to a boring meeting or deal with a difficult customer. Their bosses will be telling them what to do. When they look at the picture it reminds them that soon it will be the weekend, and eventually it will be summer.

Happiness is still there, in the picture.

So much of the time we're in a rush — we have to jostle and push our way forward if we're going to get any attention. It feels like we're always competing and trying really hard (and it doesn't always work out well).

The day sweet rationing ended, London, England, 1953

So it's good to bottle times when we feel still, calm and happy in ourselves; at those times we might feel a bit like the sculpture below. It was made in 1946 by Barbara Hepworth.* It's so balanced, solid and clean. It's smooth and brown on the outside and crisp and white on the inside. It's not trying to do anything, it's just happy being itself.

Barbara Hepworth, Pelagos, 1946

* Barbara Hepworth was one of the first women in England to become famous as an artist, because unfairly, for a long time it was only men who could have careers in art. For much of her life, Barbara Hepworth lived in a village called St Ives, in Cornwall, on the far west tip of England. Following her example, lots of other artists moved to the same village. It must have been amazing to live there: being an artist would have been quite normal rather than a bit unusual.

Works of art like these can help to remind us of our own tranquil moments.

Bottling happiness is so important because life is full of ups and downs. When things are going badly we lose touch with what's nice. We only think about what's awful and we feel that life is totally grim. But that's not really fair — it's not that life is always bad, it's just that we're forgetting the lovely bits.

When art bottles nice times and nice feelings it means we can get hold of them when things aren't so good. And when we look at the images it brings back good feelings — just like when bottling was invented, it meant people could taste the lovely sweetness of a strawberry, even in the middle of winter.

The desire to be cheerful comes from knowledge of life's difficulties.

Some adults think that 'cheerful' art can be a bit babyish. They imagine that if you like a cheerful picture — something that is simply happy — it's because you don't understand how bad the world really is. They think that cheerful pictures are just pretending everything is fine. Instead, they say, we should be concentrating on how bad everything is.

But actually, the truth is that the artists who painted some of the most cheerful pictures knew all about how hard and difficult life can be.

All through his life, Vincent van Gogh* painted lovely, cheerful pictures of flowers; he particularly liked roses.

Vincent van Gogh, *Roses*, 1890

Yet you can see from the picture he painted of himself, with a bandage round his face, that he knew a lot about suffering and sorrow. He painted nice, happy things because he needed to cheer himself up — because he knew how bad things can be. He understood that if you only feel gloomy and sad and

---

* We saw a picture of van Gogh's bedroom on page 26. Van Gogh was born in the Netherlands in 1853 into quite a wealthy family. He was a serious child and was greatly concerned for those people who didn't have well-off parents. His brother Theo was his best friend. Amazingly, during his life no one wanted to buy any of his paintings, but today any picture by him is worth an absolute fortune.

you don't try to cheer yourself up, you won't have the strength and confidence to face the difficulties of life.

Vincent van Gogh, Self-Portrait with Bandaged Ear, 1889

This is because our minds are able to do a very peculiar, but very fortunate thing. Feeling cheerful actually makes us more able to cope with our difficulties. Normally we suppose we will be cheerful when our problems are solved. But actually, if we are in a good mood we are much better at solving our problems in the first place.

Sadness

Sometimes you feel rather miserable — it's normal. Maybe a friend wasn't nice to you; the grown-ups have been having an argument (again); you wanted to get onto the swimming team but you weren't picked; someone said something mean to you at school; or you saw something horrible on the news. There are lots of reasons we can feel sad.

When you're feeling sad or upset people usually try to cheer you up. They tell you that things are going to be OK, and that you will feel better tomorrow. They mean well, but actually they're not helping. You can get the impression that you are never supposed to feel sad. That if you are unhappy or a bit miserable or feel like crying that there is something wrong with you. But art is different.

Art is a tool for helping us cope with sadness.

A lot of artists have been intrigued by sadness. They see it as an important part of life that needs to be taken seriously. One way art can help with sadness is by being quite honest and admitting that things really are a bit awful. It recognises that sometimes you should feel sad: It is a sensible, reasonable, proper thing to feel.

Here's an artist, Nicolas Poussin, who lived a long time ago.*
Sometimes he felt very sad:

Nicolas Poussin, Self-portrait, c. 1630

Poussin did this drawing of himself while looking in the mirror. He really was not at all happy that day.

* Poussin was born in 1594. His family owned a castle in France but he wanted to be a painter. In those days, painting wasn't considered a proper job for someone like him, so he ran away from home. He made a lot of mistakes and got into a lot of trouble. Then he decided to change his life. After a while, things worked out and he became a great artist. But he never forgot how hard life can be.

Nicolas Poussin, Winter or The Flood, c. 1660–1664

This is another picture Poussin painted*. It says:

Life can be grim. You are happily going through life in your little boat, and suddenly there's a terrible storm — the wind is blowing, the rain is lashing down and your boat is about to sink; the best you can hope for is that you might be able to cling to a rock… but there's a snake circling in the water.

* This painting shows a story from the Old Testament, the first book of the Bible. God gets so angry that he sends a great flood to destroy everything on Earth. Most people weren't that bad, but their world collapsed. Poussin thought this was what often happens: obviously you're not perfect, but then something unexpected happens and all the things you took for granted are washed away.

These (hopefully) aren't exactly your problems. But if you told this painting all about your own sorrows it would say:

I know, I know, that's so hard, we can be sad together.

You need someone to admit that you've got a good reason to be upset before you can think about how to put things right.

Sometimes you do not actually need to be cheered up at all — you need someone to understand and to agree that lots of things are unfair and disappointing and really very upsetting.

Perhaps that someone is your teddy bear. Some people think teddy bears are just for children. And sometimes, as they get older, children feel like they're getting too old for a teddy. But that's not right. In an important way, you will need a teddy bear all your life. Does that sound strange? Let's think about what a teddy bear really is. It's got furry ears, a tiny pointy nose and a sweet little smile. That's very nice, but these are not the most important things about a teddy bear.

The really important thing is when you feel sad or lonely or lost, a teddy bear will be there with you. A teddy bear won't ask you annoying questions, it won't tell you it's all your fault, and if you cry it won't mind. They won't say anything, but you know they understand. They stop you feeling so lonely. (You might get the same feeling with a knitted rabbit or a special blanket you rub against your nose.)

However grown-up you are there will always be times when you feel a bit sad or lonely or lost. This happens to everyone: It's part of being human.

Boris Kustodiev, Boy with teddy bear, 1907

Our society hasn't been very good at making teddy bears for adults, but there's one place that grown-ups can find something very like a teddy bear — in art.

Art is like a teddy bear.

Take the next painting for example — it isn't a very cuddly picture.* But like a teddy bear, it understands when you feel sad. It knows about feeling lonely, because it is a very lonely place far out in the frozen sea. You can see that the ice sheets in the picture have been grinding against each other, pushing up jagged ridges of ice. This picture knows all about feeling like there's too much pressure, or that everything is uncomfortable and difficult.

If a picture could cry, maybe this one would. It's silently saying that really important thing that we sometimes need to hear:

I know how you feel, I feel the same, I'm with you, I'm here.

Caspar David Friedrich, *The Sea of Ice or Polar Sea*, 1823–1824

* This is another picture by Caspar David Friedrich (page 49). Friedrich was what's called a 'Romantic' painter. It doesn't mean he went on lots of dates! In art, the word 'Romantic' means an artist who thinks that nature is sending us messages, and that if we look at nature through the eyes of an artist we can find comfort.

This piece of sculpture, made by an artist named Richard Serra, is huge and impressive.* It's not hiding away. It's not ashamed of feeling sad.

Richard Serra, Fernando Pessoa, 2007–2008

* Richard Serra, who made this sculpture, was born in San Francisco in 1938. He lived in New York when he was older. He liked making ginormous, heavy sculptures, so that when you look at them you feel small and weak. You couldn't possibly knock over this enormous slab of stone or even move it an inch.

The sculpture is a monument to a poet who lived in Portugal in the 20th century, Fernando Pessoa. This poet wrote some beautiful and sorrowful lines, such as:

I know, I alone
How much it hurts, this heart.

And:

O salty sea, so much of whose salt
Is Portugal's tears!

That's why the artist wanted to make a monument to him that would last practically forever. This work of art isn't just saying that it's OK to feel sad; it's saying something bigger: Sometimes it's important to feel sad.

Feeling sad can be a sign of sensitivity and maturity (even if you are still quite young). This art is telling us that clever, sensitive and good people feel like this sometimes. In fact, they feel like this *because* they are clever, sensitive and good. This reminds us of another big idea:

Art can be a tool to understand sadness — and also to recognise companionship.

Artists in the past used to imagine that if you were feeling lonely and lost, a special person might come along and be your friend.

This picture is telling us a story from long ago*:

Workshop of Andrea del Verrocchio, Tobias and the Angel, 1470–1475

* This picture was painted in Italy in the 1400s. It came from the workshop of Andrea del Verrocchio. He's not that well known, but was a really good teacher. He had an art school and a lot of his pupils went on to become famous artists — including Leonardo da Vinci.

A boy (he's the one wearing red trousers) is having a very difficult time. His father isn't well and the boy has to go on a long, difficult journey to get the right medicine. He gets lost and becomes scared.

The artist imagines the ideal friend who can help him: an angel, with coloured wings and a little gold circle above their head to show they're very kind. The angel understands how difficult it is, and they say encouraging things to the boy.

The angel says:

I'll be friends with you because I can see you are
feeling troubled, upset and sad. Sometimes we feel
like being friends is only about having fun together,
but a really important part of being friends is that
we can feel sad together.

In your room you have the modern versions of angels: You have your collection of things that can understand you and comfort you, whisper in your ear and be your companion.

You won't have to face the tricky parts of every day alone, because these works of art are with you, by your side.

Balance

We've looked at ways that art can be a tool for remembering, appreciation, hope and sadness. This next part of the book is about the idea of *balance*, and how art can help us with it. 'Balance' is a very interesting concept, but it is not really something people talk about a lot — probably you do not go around saying:

Oh, I wish I had more balance in my life! I wish I could find some art to help me get some more balance!

(Though you might after reading this chapter!) In order to introduce you to the idea of balance, let's look at a story about some things that happened a long time ago, between about 1800 and 1900.

At that time, there was a big change happening in a lot of countries: It was called the *Industrial Revolution*. What that means is that lots of new machines were being invented, huge factories were being built, the first railways were being made and there were many new roads and bridges and houses. Large numbers of people moved from the countryside to work in the new factories and towns. Cities got much, much bigger very quickly. Before this time, most people lived on farms or in little villages, but now nearly everyone was living in towns and cities, on streets with rows and rows of houses, with hardly any trees and usually not even a garden to sit in.

A busy London street in the 19th century

Mostly people had more money because you could get paid more for working in a factory than for working on a farm, so it wasn't all bad — but it was a big change.

What kind of art do you think was popular during the Industrial Revolution?

You might think people would want pictures of all the new factories and busy streets, or of steam trains racing through new tunnels.

But that's not what happened at all. This is the kind of art that became very popular:

Helen Allingham, A Cottage with Sunflowers at Peaslake, c. 1848-1926

What people really wanted were pictures of the things they missed: cottages, trees, flowers and quiet country lanes. They were looking for balance. This is telling us something quite important:

Art is a tool for balance.

We need art to give us the things that are missing from the rest of our lives. By doing this, looking at art can help us feel more complete.

We can use the idea of balance to help us make sense of something pretty puzzling. You will start to notice that:

People like very different things.

For example, people have very different ideas about what makes a kitchen nice.

A cosy kitchen

For some people, this is what they'd like a kitchen to look like. Why might that be? It's probably because it looks relaxed and cosy and like it doesn't matter if you make a bit of a mess. That's very appealing if you feel that in other parts of your life (at school or at work), you have to concentrate hard, try to get everything right and be on your best behaviour all the time. This kitchen balances the demanding, formal bits of life.

If your dad likes this kitchen, it might be because he feels everyone is making too many demands on him (poor Dad!).

People like the things that are missing from their lives. They like the things that restore balance. What if this is someone's perfect kitchen?

A modern kitchen

In this kitchen, everything is totally under control, clean and beautifully organised. So why might someone really like that? Imagine if the rest of their life was a bit chaotic: they are always in a rush, they have got a laptop in one hand, their car keys in another, they're trying to arrange a business meeting at the same time as checking Granny's OK and making sure their child is wearing a warm coat (it's a cold day) and they need to check there are enough eggs in the fridge to make an omelette. (This could be someone's mum!) This kitchen shows what's missing from their life — that's why they like it.

We can ask the same questions about pictures. What kind of person might really like this picture?* What might they feel is missing in their life?

Raffaello Sanzio, The School of Athens, 1509–1511

Suppose they feel that people do not pay enough attention to ideas; they feel like everyone just chats about silly things all the time. This picture would be lovely for them because it shows everyone talking about important things, listening carefully and thinking deeply.

---

* This fresco was done by Raffaello Sanzio, also known as Raphael. For a long time, people thought he was the best artist who ever lived (though not so many people feel this way today). The picture shows a selection of the cleverest people who had ever lived up to that point. They actually lived at different times and in different places, but Raphael imagined them all meeting up and talking together. Imagine hiding in the corner and listening to what they were saying.

Suppose someone feels like too many people are noisy and showing off and trying to be the centre of attention. They might really like this painting because it's a very quiet, calm picture; it's happy just to stay in the background and watch what's going on.*

Giorgio Morandi, Natura Morta, 1953

People like different things, because different things are missing in each person's life.

* Giorgio Morandi was born in Bologna, Italy in 1890 and lived there his whole life. He didn't really care about selling his paintings, he just painted things that he liked and that meant a lot to him. To his surprise, he discovered that they meant a lot to other people as well. What he loved most was going around his house and collecting jars and bottles that he liked, putting them on a table and spending hours just copying how the light and shadows fell on them.

Now let's ask some quite personal questions: What might be missing in your life? What kind of balance do you need? A good way to find out is to ask another question:

What do you like looking at?

Suppose you like this:

A picture of a colony on Mars

It is pretty amazing to have a whole city under a huge glass cover. There aren't any cities like that on Earth. There is a sense of adventure: You're going to a new place.

Remember we've been saying that we often like things because they pick up on something that's missing in our lives. You like an exciting picture about an unknown place because you feel like your life isn't exciting enough. The excitement in the picture perhaps makes up for the lack of excitement you normally feel.

This tells you about what you might like in art. You might like art that's exciting and fantastical; that imagines new worlds and places.

This picture is about people trying to build a tower so high that they'd actually be able to reach the sky and find out what was beyond it! Of course, they didn't succeed.* But it was a fantastic ambition. You can imagine how they were thinking, that if only they could build a bit higher, they might get there:

Pieter Bruegel the Elder, The Tower of Babel, 1563

* The story of people wanting to build towers that reach to the sky is an old one. Imagine before there were aeroplanes or telescopes — people didn't know how far away the sky actually was. It looks like it could be close, but actually the sky has lots of layers of air and you can't touch it all. Building a tower isn't going to help. Beyond our atmosphere, there's nothing immediately exciting: just a few rocks, the odd satellite and miles of emptiness before you get to the moon.

Or if you like pictures about adventure, you might like this*:

Caspar David Friedrich, The Wanderer Above the Sea of Fog, c.1817–1818

If you were in this picture you could do whatever you want — no one is going to tell you what to do and you don't have to fit in with other people, you can just go off on an adventure on your own.

* This is another painting by Caspar David Friedrich (from pages 49 and 95). Unusually, we're seeing this character from behind, when most paintings show us people's faces. From this viewpoint, we can imagine it's us standing there on the craggy mountaintop, looking over the mist and fog into the distance.

Or maybe instead of those things, you like looking at this:

A footballer about to score a goal

It's a great picture. It shows someone who is powerful. They can do exciting things and make things happen — they can score a goal and lead their team to victory — and that might appeal a lot if at the moment you don't feel very powerful; if you feel you can't influence things or make anything happen. Your brain notices what's missing and gets excited when it sees the missing piece reflected in a picture.

In a gallery you might feel the same way when you look at the next picture.* It shows a powerful person who can make things happen. He tells the whole army what to do and makes big decisions — he is the leader. He might win a big battle.

Those could be exciting ideas if you have to spend a lot of your life at school and you don't feel like you're charge of much in your life.

Jacques-Louis David, Napoleon Crossing the Alps or Bonaparte at the St Bernard Pass, c. 1800–1801

* This painting is by the French artist Jacques-Louis David. It is of his hero, the most ambitious political leader of the 19th century, Napoleon Bonaparte. When he was still in his twenties, Napoleon lead his army through the Alps, which everyone thought was impossible. The artist has painted Napoleon pointing the way forward, saying, 'Let's go right over the mountains!'

Or, maybe you're not into sports and power or discovering new worlds. Instead, you might be excited by this:

A Jaguar automobile

It feels very glamorous and elegant — and maybe your life doesn't feel like that at all.

But you might be able to feel something similar when you look at this very old statue on the next page.* It's glamorous and elegant, too. There's a feeling of lightness and ease, of controlled strength, victory and triumph. It's not surprising that we get excited by flashy cars and grand statues in a competitive world where so often we're on the losing side.

* This very old statue was made in ancient Greece, over two thousand years ago. It used to have a head and arms, but someone knocked them off centuries ago. The Greek name of the figure is Nike, who was their goddess of victory — that's where the sportswear brand took their name from.

Winged Victory or Nike of Samothrace, c. 200-190 BCE

Art can seem very different to the kinds of things you normally enjoy looking at.

But actually, there's a secret connection. The things you like are the things that bring balance to your life: They make up for what's missing. And it is the same with the right works of art. They do the same work, helping you to feel a bit more complete just by being nearby.

113

Making sense of money

When you were little, you probably didn't think about money all that much. But as you grow up you start to realise that money is one of the driving forces of the adult world. Nearly all adults think about money every day.

Money can be extremely useful: It builds modern schools and hospitals; it's why there are lots of phones and fridges and other useful things; it's why you can order a pizza, go on holiday, have a bath or watch a film. Without lots of money moving around the world none of these things would happen.

But sometimes we get a bit confused about money. One problem starts with an obvious fact: Lots of nice things are very expensive.

When we think about these things, our brains make an unfortunate mistake — though it is an easy one to make. We start to think that *only* expensive things can be exciting, and that if something is cheap then it must be boring and a bit disappointing.

When things are expensive, we pay them a lot of attention. We notice what's great about them, because we think if something costs a lot then it must have a high value. And if something doesn't cost much, we don't pay much attention. Art can help us with this problem, because:

A lot of art is impressed by things that don't cost very much and pays those things a lot of attention.

This isn't a fancy place to live at all. If the people who lived here had a lot of money they would get someone to fix the pole holding up the climbing plant, or maybe they'd just go and live in a bigger house in another part of the city.*

Pieter de Hooch, *The Courtyard of a House in Delft*, 1658

* Pieter de Hooch, who painted this, was born in the Netherlands in 1629. His father was a bricklayer, which may help to explain why he painted every single brick in this picture so carefully. He was quite poor all his life. He particularly loved painting pictures of people just doing ordinary things at home.

But the artist liked this place exactly the way it was — that's why he spent a long time painting a picture of it. He loved this little courtyard, with its funny little door in the wall; he liked the old wooden bucket and the broom that were used to brush the bricks every day. The family liked sitting out there on sunny days; maybe it's where the little girl took her first steps not very long after her first birthday.

Francisco de Zurbarán was really excited by very ordinary kinds of fruit: Just lemons and oranges, which don't cost very much at all.* Today, hardly anyone goes around saying:

You will never believe how lucky I am,
I've got an orange and I'm going to eat it.

Francisco de Zurbarán, *Still Life with Lemons, Oranges and a Rose*, 1633

* Francisco de Zurbarán was born in 1598. In his paintings he specialised in making objects stand out clearly against a dark background. His parents were poor but eventually Francisco became the King of Spain's favourite painter.

But maybe we should, because actually an orange is an amazing thing: It's just that we forget that it is amazing because it's cheap. If we look at a work of art like this, we start to remember. Art is showing us something important here — it helps us to love ordinary things.

If we only focus on expensive things we are going to be unhappy because mostly we can't afford them. But art shows us that there are lots of wonderful things in the world that don't cost much — and that is very good news for our lives.

Art is advertising for what we really need.

Let's think for a moment about something that seems like it might be the opposite of art: *advertising*. You've seen millions of adverts in your life — but what is an advert trying to do? Basically, an advert suggests that you should buy something to solve a problem. It might be saying:

Are you unhappy with your shoes?
Buy these shoes instead.
Are you worried about your hair?
Buy this special shampoo; it will make your hair look nice.
Are you bored?
Play this game.

You might think there are adverts for everything, but actually that's not true. There are lots of important and wonderful things that normal advertising doesn't talk about at all.

Works of art are often like adverts: They are trying to get you interested in something and show you how it could help you. But usually the things that artworks are trying to 'sell' you don't actually cost anything. In the 19th century, a Danish artist called Christen Købke made lots of adverts for the sky.*

Christen Købke, *View of Østerbro from Dosseringen*, 1838

You can't buy the sky, but Købke wanted you to notice it, and be interested in looking at it. He thought if we spent more time looking at the sky our lives would be better. Maybe he was right. When you look at the clouds in the sky you stop bothering so much about the little problems of life — you feel more free (at least for a little while).

* Christen Købke was born in Denmark, and he started studying to be an artist when he was only twelve years old. He painted some very beautiful pictures but he was not very successful in selling them during his own lifetime. It is only quite recently that he's been properly appreciated as a painter.

This painting is an advert for staring out of the window*:

Gustave Caillebotte, Young Man at His Window, 1875

* Gustave Caillebotte was born in 1848, in Paris. He painted this picture in his apartment in that same city. The man standing at the window is his younger brother, who he was very fond of. Caillebotte studied law and engineering but later decided he wanted to be an artist. He enjoyed gardening and sailing, and was very good friends with Renoir, the painter we met earlier (see page 84).

It doesn't cost anything to stare out of the window. If you spent a lot of time staring out of the window at school people might laugh at you or the teacher might get angry, but this art-advert is saying that staring out the window can be great, and you should give it a try. It means you're noticing the world outside and (even more importantly) it gives you the chance to notice what's going on at the back of your own mind: interesting, unusual and important thoughts start to emerge.

This drawing is an advert for being quiet*:

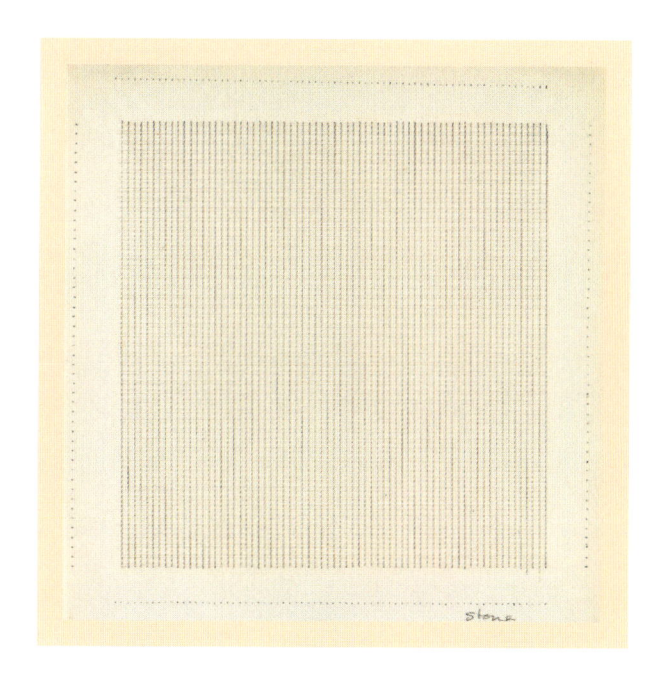

Agnes Martin, Stone, 1964

* Agnes Martin was born in Canada in 1912, but she lived most of her life in America. She enjoyed being alone. She chose to live far away from the cities, in the countryside, where she built herself a very nice house made of mud. She made lots of pictures like this one: carefully drawing each line by hand.

Normally, people who make a lot of noise get more attention. If you are quiet people might think you are boring. However, Martin's picture is saying that actually, it's quite lovely to be quiet; it's suggesting that maybe you need more quietness in your life — and there are definitely other people who need to 'buy' more quietness in their lives!

This sculpture is an advert for listening*:

Buddhist statue of Guanyin, Shanxi province, China, Jin dynasty, 1115–1234

* This statue was made in China nearly a thousand years ago. It represents a Buddhist figure called Guanyin, also known as the Goddess of Mercy. Guanyin was famous for her compassion: When someone was in trouble or feeling sad she'd be kind to them and help them.

The statue is saying:

You can bring me your worries and problems.
I'll listen and I won't jump to any conclusions.
Tell me more, let me know what is bothering you.

That's very different to what normally happens: Usually people don't listen to each other very much or very carefully. That's a huge pity. We really need to advertise listening: We need other people to hear what we have to say, and they need us to listen to them, too.

Ordinary advertising tries to persuade us to buy things, but art makes adverts for good things that can happen inside our own heads, for free: things like how we feel about ourselves, how we feel about other people, and what we think is important and valuable.

What's going on inside our heads, rather than what we buy, makes the biggest difference for our happiness.

Another tricky thing about money is how it is shared out. Some people have a lot of money and other people don't have very much at all.

Often, our society is impressed by people who make a lot of money: We think they must be great. And sometimes they are.

But this means we also tend to think that if someone doesn't have much money, they can't be much good. We might feel sorry for them, but we don't usually admire them.

However, some art is very impressed by people who don't have a lot of money. This woman hasn't got much money. Her job is making lace. In the days when this picture was painted you couldn't make much money making lace.*

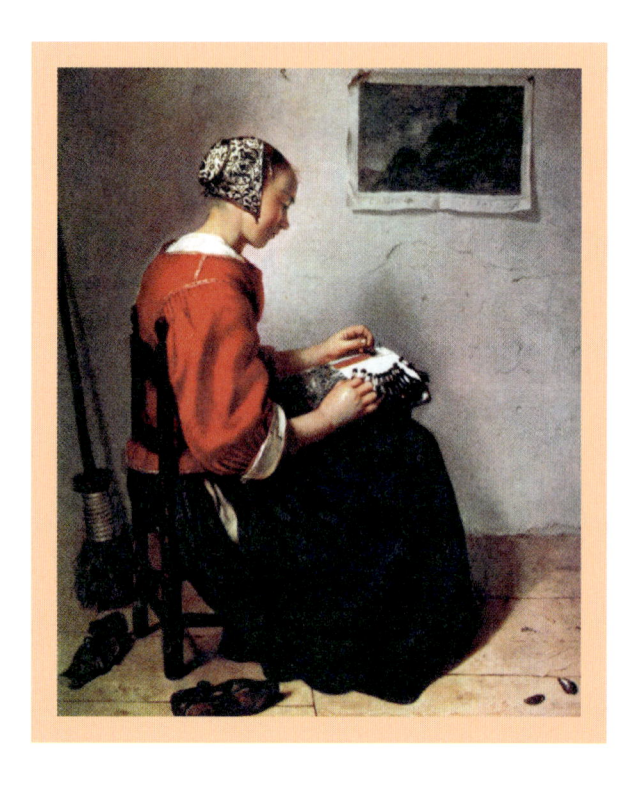

Caspar Netscher, The Lace Maker, 1662

* Caspar Netscher was going to be a doctor, but he was so good at drawing that his friends encouraged him to become an artist. He became successful, and kings bought his paintings. Later he became ill and had to stay in bed, so he had his paints brought into his bedroom so he could continue to paint.

Not many people would have been interested in her; they would think she wasn't worth paying attention to because she's poor. But the artist has a very different idea. He thinks she is wonderful. She has a kind, thoughtful face; she is patient and gentle. She's skilful with her hands. She might be lovely to talk to, and she'd probably be a good friend — if you made a joke she'd laugh even if it wasn't funny, just because she wants you to be happy. It's not her fault if she's poor.

Have you ever seen someone asking for money in the street? It can be quite upsetting.

Jacques-Louis David, Belisarius Begging for Alms, 1781

The old man with the white beard in this picture (with his grandson standing next to him) is asking people to help him. He hasn't got any money or anywhere to live.*

But let's take a closer look at him:

Detail from: Jacques-Louis David, Belisarius Begging for Alms, 1781

126

He used to be very important. He was in charge of the army — you can see a little bit of his armour poking out from under his cloak on his shoulder — and he had plenty of money. He was famous and a lot of people admired him, but then he was very unlucky. It wasn't his fault, but he lost everything.

The picture is reminding us about a big idea: *inequality.*

It might not be someone's fault if they don't have any money — a very good person can end up in a very difficult situation. When you see someone who is poor or disadvantaged, you might not realise what their life used to be like.

These artists are looking carefully at people who have no money and seeing what's good about them. They are not suggesting it's nice to be poor; they are just saying that someone can be poor and admirable and nice all at the same time — and that's a very important concept.

---

* This is another painting by Jacques-Louis David (remember he painted the picture of Napoleon on horseback pointing to the mountains on page 111). The picture is in the 'classical' style, which means that the position of every detail is very carefully thought out. For instance, the old man's right hand is exactly in the middle of the picture.

Conclusion

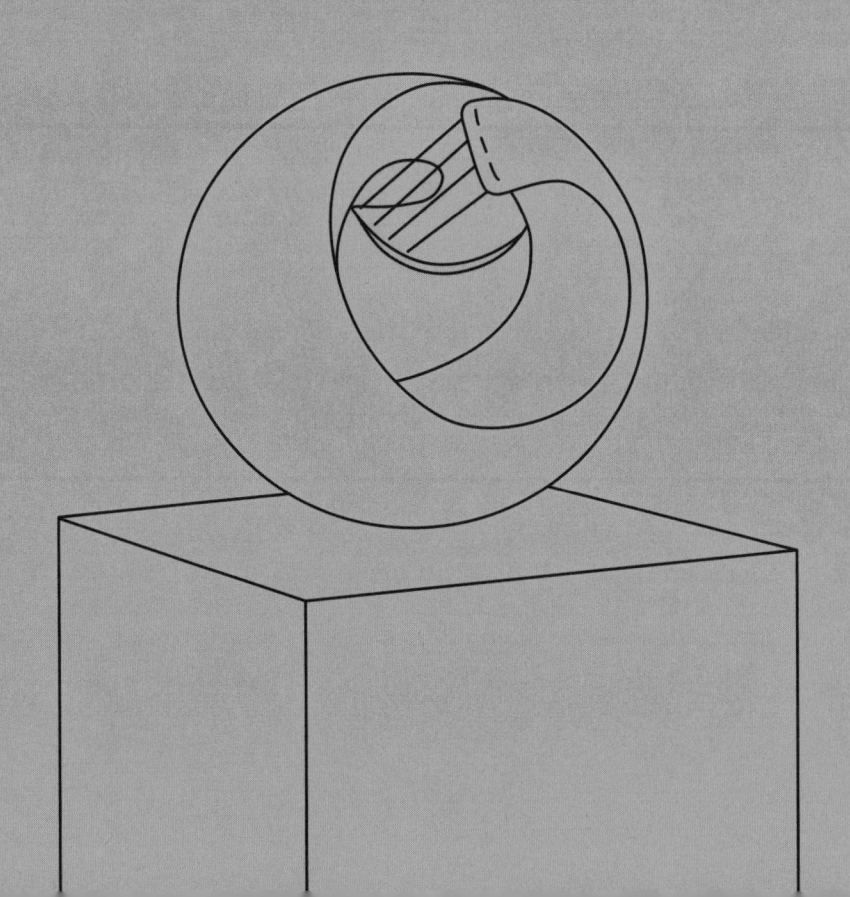

You've been trailing around the gallery for what feels like ages. Now, at last, it's time to go home. But before you leave you pass through the gift shop. A lot of people think that the gift shop is just there to make some money for the gallery — but actually this is the most important part of your visit.

That's because the shop is asking you a really good question:

What do you want to take home with you from the gallery?

A lot of the art probably didn't interest you much, but maybe there were one or two things that intrigued you. So how do you transport those nice things into your life?*

If the gift shop could speak it would say something like this:

I'm glad you liked looking at a picture of some rocks in gallery XI at 3.14 p.m. today, and at the picture of clouds in the big room with the green walls at 3.57 p.m., but it might be years before you come back. It would be great if the things you've enjoyed in art could be part of your everyday life. What can I do to make that happen?

The shop is *asking* a great question, but mostly it isn't very good at *answering* it.

---

* We're not recommending coming back in the middle of the night with a van, climbing in a back window and carting off a couple of priceless masterpieces!

The shop might suggest you buy a mug — or maybe a tea towel — with the name of a famous artist on it.

The gift shop at Asia Museum of Modern Art, Taiwan

That could be quite fun. But it's not really helping you to take the experience you had when looking at the art home with you. It's not really the artist's name that matters, but what they were saying to you through their art — and the mug and the tea towel don't seem to know anything about that.

Actually, the most important things in the gift shop are the postcards on sale. Some people find that quite a surprising thing to say. A postcard is usually the cheapest thing in the shop while the actual work itself might cost as much as ten or even a hundred houses. The original was carefully created, by hand, by a genius with paints, brushes, pencils or clay, while the card was churned out by a machine in a factory.

But a postcard is a wonderful thing: You can hold it in your hand, you can press your nose up to it to look at a detail or you can put it on the floor and lie down beside it — and the postcard is sending you exactly the same message as the real artwork when you saw it in the gallery.

Remember we've been saying that works of art are always sending us messages. They might be saying:

An apple can be lovely.
Looking at the sky helps you calm down.
Someone who doesn't have much money might be lovely.

But probably, the time when you most need to hear those messages is not when you are in the gallery. Galleries are really bad at timing. The artworks in them might be sending you messages that are really useful — but they are sending them at the wrong time. Postcards solve this problem because you can keep them in your room, in your own private gallery, and they are around to help you whenever you need them.

Let's see how this works (to take just one example, though there are many) when you are feeling shy...

It's not very nice feeling shy: You feel awkward and you are worried that someone's going to ask you something that you don't know the answer to; or you feel you are supposed to say something, but you don't know what. Your skin gets hot and maybe you feel like you might start to cry.

There's a postcard that could help*. The man on the left (the one wearing the orange tights) is a very important person — the Spanish ambassador.

Jean-Auguste-Dominique Ingres, Henry IV Receiving the Spanish Ambassador, 1817

The Spanish ambassador has come there to meet an even more important person — the King of France, who normally looked like he does in the picture on the next page.

* This is what's called a 'historical picture'. It shows an event from around 1600, a long time before it was painted, in 1817. The artist, Jean-Auguste-Dominique Ingres, wanted to show that kings were real people too. They too could feel sad, or stub their toe, or burp, or enjoy playing with their children. Ingres wanted to show that someone could be nice and kind as well as powerful and important.

Jacques Boulbene, Henry IV, King of France and Navarre, c. 1600

But the ambassador got a big surprise. Instead of striding around in his armour or sitting on a throne with his crown on, the king was crawling around the room pretending to be a horse, while his children were riding on his back. They were having a great time.

This is an important thing to think about, because usually when we feel shy it's because we are only considering what the other person looks like just at that moment.

Maybe just now they look very imposing, or different to us, or clever or serious. But if we could see them at other times we'd realise they have lots of alternative, more human sides to them. They can be funny and silly and really quite a lot like us. If we remembered that, we wouldn't feel so worried about talking to them, and we wouldn't feel so shy.

This can sometimes happen if your mum or dad run into one of their friends when you are out, or if they come round for dinner. You look at this strange person who you don't know and you can't think of anything to say. If you often get shy, try looking at a postcard of this picture and thinking about the ways that people who make you feel shy might be silly.

The important thing is that the useful message that the painting is relaying isn't stuck in the gallery. You can take a postcard home and use it whenever you need it.

Now let's consider another one of our big ideas to do with art and objects:

Are you being 'materialistic'?

What does 'materialistic' mean? 'Materialistic' is quite an odd word and maybe it's not one you've used much, but you probably know about the idea that it represents. Adults use it when they want to say that someone cares too much about physical things. If someone is materialistic, it suggests they care more about their car or their house or having a fancy watch or clothes than they care about their friends or being kind to people. They're too interested in their possessions and showing them off.

From this, it sounds like if you are interested in material 'stuff' then you can't also be interested in ideas, feelings or kindness — we could call these other things 'soul stuff'.*

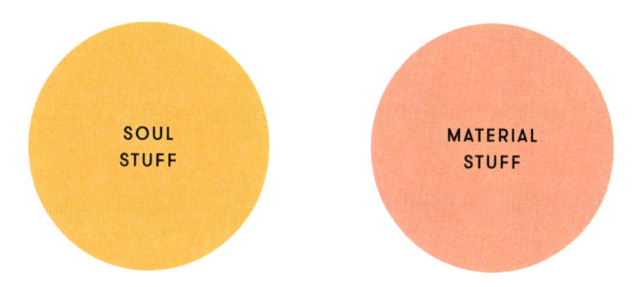

SOUL STUFF   MATERIAL STUFF

But actually, there can be an overlap: Sometimes the right material stuff is closely connected to important soul stuff.

SOUL STUFF   MATERIAL STUFF
↑
GOOD MATERIALISM

---

* 'Soul' is a useful word for talking about your sense of 'being you': your thoughts, feelings, ideas, hopes, worries, longings and memories; your experiences of love and happiness or sadness; your friendships and interests. All these things are inside you: They make up your 'soul'.

The overlap isn't by accident. It's there for a good reason:

Material things can help us with love and being nice and with friendship and kindness.

Let's look at an example of this happening. This is a plate that belonged to some people living in England at the start of the 20th century:

Duncan Grant, A Painted Pottery Dish, c. 1930

These people lived in the countryside and often had interesting friends over to stay. They wrote books, painted pictures and had long conversations. They cared a lot about 'soul stuff'.

136

This is a picture of them. They were known as 'The Bloomsbury Set' and they were a group of writers, artists and intellectuals from the first half of the 20th century.

The Bloomsbury Set at Charleston farmhouse, in Sussex, England

Obviously they needed to have plates to put food on. Imagine putting a pile of spaghetti straight onto the table! But a plate can do lots of other things as well. What else?

The plate looks cheerful. It's colourful, with lots of bright yellow, like sunshine, so if you're not in a very good mood when you sit down to dinner it can cheer you up. It's a big plate, too: It's not just for one person, rather it's for putting things on that everyone can share — it's generous.

And look at the curved edge:

Detail from: Duncan Grant, A Painted Pottery Dish, c. 1930

Each curve flows into the other; there's lots of movement, but all the movement fits together. Imagine a conversation with someone that went like this: You say something (one curve) and they say something else (another curve), but it meets your curve very nicely — then you do it again. It's an interesting thought: The shape of the plate is a bit like the shape of a nice conversation. It is a very personal plate as well. In the middle there is a picture of a basket of flowers; the flowers were collected from their garden, and the basket was a present from a friend.

It is a plate, but it's not *just* a plate; it is also talking to the people who own it about friendship and sharing and happiness. It is material stuff, but it is also soul stuff too.

You can understand why it might be good to actually buy a plate like this: It's a good possession to have. In a way it is materialistic to want to buy it — after all, the plate is 'stuff', just like a new pair of trainers or a TV. But it's not the bad kind of materialism that's just about showing off or having lots of things you don't need. In fact, it's the opposite.

Often people think art just means pictures and statues, but now we're seeing that a plate can be a work of art as well. Not because it's in a museum, but because it does the same thing as other works of art:

Art is a tool for reminding us about soul-stuff.

This isn't just a story about some people who lived a long time ago and had a nice plate. It's also a story about *you*. Maybe you wouldn't particularly want that exact plate. But one day you will buy some plates (practically every adult has to buy some plates at some point in their life). In fact, you'll be buying a lot of things.

This is the grown-up version of what we've been talking about before: choosing what posters you would like in your ideal room. Now we're imagining all the other things you might get at some point, but it's very much part of the same conversation because these other things can be art as well.

What things would be in your ideal room?

'Good materialism' involves thinking about lots of ordinary possessions and asking what each one could mean to you.

Let's think about chairs, for instance. If you don't want to sit on the floor, you're going to need a chair. But there are lots of kinds of chairs. So, what sort of chair would you choose?

A chair can be a work of art: It sends you messages about what's important to you. And every chair sends a different message. When you are choosing a chair you are really trying to choose what message it would be good for you to hear.

This chair is talking about being alert and upright; you can't really slouch in it. It's straightforward:

Stickback Windsor Chair, 18th century

You can see exactly how it was made; it wants you to get things organised and get some work done. Maybe that's the kind of encouragement you sometimes need!

This chair is more interested in dignity and formality (it's a little bit like a throne):

French Wing Back Chair, 19th century

It says people should listen to what you say — which might be good if you can be a little hesitant about saying what you really believe.

Here's a chair that's comfortable but very unfussy:

Ludwig Mies van der Rohe, The Barcelona® Chair, 1929

It invites you to lean back, listen and think. It's saying:

Don't rush, get things clear in your own head before you act, don't worry too much about what other people think, make your own decisions.

It doesn't need to be a chair; it could be something simple and inexpensive.

Forks can be art too.

Cutlery is another thing that you will definitely buy at some point in your life (though you might prefer to use chopsticks).

A simple fork

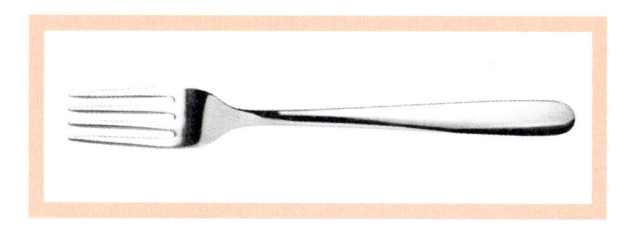

This fork is very simple and efficient: It doesn't want to be complicated or fancy or make a fuss.

An elaborate fork

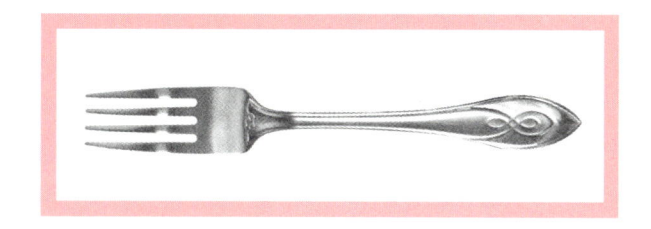

This fork is more rounded and elaborate. It likes making clear distinctions: Each part is separate, with the top part coming to a definite end before the narrow middle section and finally the curved end. It doesn't like muddling things up.

A decorative fork

This fork is happy being unusual; it's decorative and does not mind being complicated. Sometimes you might worry about standing out from the crowd, because it can feel lonely to be different. But this fork is saying something rather kind and useful:

Don't worry too much — I'm different too,
and we can be different together.

You can see how even something that seems as obvious and normal as a fork can be sending messages to us like art — it has an opinion about what's nice or important. And just by choosing which fork you like, you can decide what messages you want to have in your life every time you eat your dinner.

Maybe it seems strange to be talking about chairs and forks in a book about art. But actually it makes good sense.

Art is an object that sends you an important, helpful message about your life.

Sometimes this helpful message might come from a picture or a statue, but it could equally come from an 'ordinary' thing like a cup or a bag, a table or a spoon. What is important is that across your life you gradually surround yourself with the images and objects that help you become the best version of yourself — even if that's quite different from other people.

To speak very grandly for a moment, the aim of civilisation is that all the material, physical things we own or use should help our souls. They should encourage us to be kinder, more patient, more confident, more forgiving, more understanding of other people and of ourselves, calmer, clearer about what is really important to us and better able to cope with the unavoidable difficulties of being alive.

Edvard Munch, The Scream, 1910

The right things have a good influence on us — and that is important, because so often we don't feel kind or forgiving or patient or good at coping.

And finally…

A lot of adults think that art belongs in art galleries and in museums. That's understandable because that's where the most famous art is kept. But it is also a mistake. (One of the tricky things you learn as you grow up is that adults can quite often be wrong about important things.)

Alma Thomas, *Elysian Fields*, 1973

What we are saying is that art doesn't really belong in art galleries at all. It really belongs in your life.

Art is important to you because it helps you.

It won't be all art that helps you — just some. You're starting out on a life-long project to find the few works of art that mean the most to you. Eventually you'll find ones you need.

Henri Rousseau, *Myself: Portrait-Landscape*, 1890

And maybe when you are older, in ten years time or so, you will remember this book and feel it's helped you. That's what we hope.

Image References

Cover	*Pelagos*: Barbara Hepworth © Bowness, *Stone*: © Agnes Martin / DACS 2020
p. 2	Strekalova / Shutterstock
p. 3	Judith Kerr, illustration from *The Tiger Who Came to Tea*, 1968. Image © Kerr-Kneale Productions Ltd 1968. Reprinted by permission of HarperCollins Publishers Ltd.
p. 4	U.Ozel.Images / iStockphoto
p. 5	Andrea del Sarto, *Madonna of the Harpies*, 1517. Oil on canvas, 207 cm × 178 cm. Uffizi Gallery, Florence, Italy. / Wikimedia Commons
p. 6	Constantin Brancusi, *Fish*, 1926. Bronze, metal and wood, 93 cm × 50 cm × 50 cm. Tate Gallery, London, England. © Succession Brancusi. All rights reserved. ADAGP, Paris and DACS London 2020.
p. 7	AC Almelor / Unsplash
p. 10	Tobias A. Müller / Unsplash
p. 11	Bachelot Pierre J-P / Wikimedia Commons (CC BY-SA 3.0)
p. 12(tl)	Photo © RMN-Grand Palais / Wikimedia Commons
p. 12(tm)	Guillermo Kalho, *Frida Kahlo*, 1932. Gelatin silver print, 15.2 cm × 10.8 cm. Sotheby's / Wikimedia Commons
p. 12(tr)	National Archives and Records Administration / (NAID) 175147 Wikimedia Commons
p. 12(bl)	Nadar, *Portrait of Claude Monet*, 1899 / Wikimedia Commons
p. 12(bm)	Alfred Stieglitz, *Georgia O'Keeffe*, 1930. Gelatin silver print. 24.1 cm × 18.8 cm. Metropolitan Museum of Art, New York, USA. Accession number: 1997.61.43. Gift of Georgia O'Keeffe, through the generosity of The Georgia O'Keeffe Foundation and Jennifer and Joseph Duke, 1997.
p. 12(br)	Yayoi Kusama, Person of Cultural Merit, received the Order of Culture, 2016. Licensed under the Government of Japan Standard Terms of Use (Ver.2.0) / Wikimedia Commons
p. 13(l)	University of Glasgow / Wikimedia Commons
p. 13(m)	Wikimedia Commons / Public domain
p. 13(r)	Harris & Ewing, photographer. *"Lady Edison" with latest invention*, 1927. Library of Congress, Washington D.C., USA. Gift; Harris & Ewing, Inc. 1955. / Wikimedia Commons
p. 15	Mural: Robert T. McCall. National Air and Space Museum, Smithsonian, Washington. Photo: Carol M. Highsmith Archive, Library of Congress, Prints and Photographs Division. Gift and purchase; Carol M. Highsmith; 2011; (DLC/PP-2011:124). Forms part of the Selects Series in the Carol M. Highsmith Archive.
p. 17	Mitchell Luo / Unsplash
p. 18(tl)	Ermess / Shutterstock
p. 18(tr)	Adam Pretty / Getty Images
p. 18(bl)	Dougal Waters / Getty Images
p. 18(br)	Chris McGrath / Getty Images
p. 19	B.O'Kane / Alamy Stock Photo
p. 20	Arcaid Images / Alamy Stock Photo
p. 22	Anthony Van Dyck, *Charles I (1600–1649) with M. de St Antoine*, 1633. Oil on canvas, 370 cm × 270 cm. Queen's Gallery, Windsor Castle, England. / Wikimedia Commons
p. 23	Titian, *Clarissa Strozzi (1540–1581)*, 1542. Oil on canvas, 115 cm × 98 cm. Gemäldegalerie, Berlin, Germany. Artexplorer / Alamy Stock Photo
p. 24	Joseph Mallord William Turner, *Ulysses deriding Polyphemus*, 1829. Oil on canvas, 132.5 cm × 203 cm. National Gallery, London, England. Turner Bequest, 1856. / Wikimedia Commons
p. 25	Vincent van Gogh, *Portrait of Eugène Boch*, 1888. Oil on canvas, 60 cm × 45 cm. Musee D'Orsay, Paris, France. Peter Barritt / Alamy Stock Photo
p. 26	Vincent van Gogh, *Bedroom*, 1888. Oil on canvas, 72.4 cm × 91.3 cm. Van Gogh Museum, Amsterdam, the Netherlands (Vincent van Gogh Foundation). / Wikimedia Commons
p. 27	Mary Beale, *Sketch of the Artist's Son, Bartholomew Beale, Facing Left*, c. 1660. Oil paint on paper, 32.5 cm × 24.5 cm. Tate Museum, London, England.

	Purchased 2010. Asar Studios / Alamy Stock Photo
p. 28	Jean Carlo Emer / Unsplash
p. 31	kevin laminto / Unsplash
p. 33	Christian Fregnan / Unsplash
p. 34/37	Claude Lorrain, *Landscape with David at the Cave of Adullam*, 1658. Oil on canvas. 112 cm × 185 cm. National Gallery, London, England. Holwell Carr Bequest, 1831. / Wikimedia Commons
p. 39	Jean-François Millet, *The Wood Sawyers*, 1850-1852. Oil on canvas, 57 cm × 81 cm. Victoria and Albert Museum, London, England. Bequeathed by Constantine Alexander Ionides. / Wikimedia Commons
p.40(t)	Charles Deluvio / Unsplash
p.40(m)	Ocean Ng / Unsplash
p.40(b)	British Library / Unsplash
p. 42	John Singer Sargent, *The Birthday Party*, 1887. Oil on canvas, 61 cm × 73.7 cm. Minneapolis Institute of Arts, Minneapolis, USA. The Ethel Morrison Van Derlip Fund and the John R. Van Derlip Fund. / Wikimedia Commons
p. 45	Jean-Baptiste Regnault, *The Origin of Painting: Dibutades Tracing the Portrait of a Shepherd*, 1785. Oil on canvas, 120 cm × 140 cm. Musée National du Château, Versailles, France. The Picture Art Collection / Alamy Stock Photo
p. 46	Thomas Gainsborough, *The Painter's Daughters chasing a Butterfly*, c. 1756. Oil on canvas, 113.5 cm × 105 cm. National Gallery, London, England. Henry Vaughan Bequest, 1900. / Wikimedia Commons
p. 47	Sakarin Sawasdinaka / Shutterstock
p. 48	Hasegawa Tōhaku, *Pine Trees / left hand screen*, 16th century. Pair of six-folded screens; ink on paper, 156.8 cm × 356 cm. Tokyo National Museum, Tokyo, Japan. / Wikimedia Commons
p. 49	Caspar David Friedrich, *The Grosse Gehege near Dresden*, c. 1832. Oil on canvas, 73.5 cm × 103 cm. Galerie Neue Meister, Dresden, Germany. Acquired in 1909 from Ella von Nostitz and Jänckendorf, Joachimstein Abbey near Radmeritz. / Wikimedia Commons
p. 50	Hilaire-Germain-Edgar Degas, *Beach Scene*, c. 1869-1870. Oil on paper mounted on canvas, 47.5 cm × 82.9 cm. National Gallery, London, England. Sir Hugh Lane Bequest, 1917. / Wikimedia Commons
p. 52	Cy Twombly, *Untitled*, 2000-2001. Acrylic, paint, pencil on handmade paper unbound in linen slip, 57 cm × 76 cm © Cy Twombly Foundation. Courtesy Gagosian.
p. 53	Lia_t / Shutterstock
p. 55	French School (15th century). *Dame Fortune and victims falling from her wheel, from Boccaccio's 'The Fall of Princes'*, 1467 (vellum). © Bridgeman Art Library.
p. 56	Berthe Morisot, *In a Park*, c.1874. Pastel on paper, 91.8 cm × 72.5 cm. Musée du Petit Palais, Paris, France. © Bridgeman Art Library.
p. 59	Albrecht Dürer, *Great Piece of Turf*, 1503. Watercolour, 40.8 cm × 31.5 cm. Albertina, Vienna, Austria. / Wikimedia Commons
p. 60	Pablo Picasso, *Tête de taureau (Bull's Head)*, 1942. Bicycle seat and handlebars (leather and metal), 33.5 cm × 43.5 cm × 19 cm. Musée National Picasso, Paris, France. © Succession Picasso/DACS, London 2020. Copyright management. Photo © RMN-Grand Palais (Musée national Picasso-Paris) / Béatrice Hatala
p. 62	Wolfgang Lutz / Unsplash
p. 63	Photographieundmehr / Dreamstime
p. 64	John Ruskin, *Fast sketch of withered oak*, 1879. Watercolour, bodycolor and ink, 14 cm × 18 cm. Guild of St. George Collection, The Ruskin Gallery, Cambridge, England. / Wikimedia Commons
p. 66	Marco Verch / Flickr (CC BY 2.0)
p. 67	D de Vosthem, *Les Ages de l'homme (The Ages of Man)*, 16th century. Engraving on paper, 29.5 cm × 40.6 cm. The British Museum, London, England. © The Trustees of the British Museum.
p. 68(tl)	Rembrandt, *Self-Portrait*, c. 1629. Oil on panel, 44.4 cm × 34.2 cm. The Clowes Fund Collection, Indianapolis Museum of Art, Indianapolis, USA. Courtesy of The Clowes Fund. / Wikimedia Commons
p. 68(tr)	Rembrandt, *Self-Portrait in a Flat Cap*, 1642. Oil on panel, 70.4 cm × 58.8 cm.

	Royal Collection, London, England. / Wikimedia Commons
p. 68(bl)	Rembrandt, *Self-Portrait*, 1652. Oil on canvas, 112 cm × 81.5 cm.
	Kunsthistorisches Museum, Vienna, Austria. / Wikimedia Commons
p. 68(br)	Rembrandt, *Self-Portrait with Two Circles*, c. 1665–1669. Oil on panel, 114.3 cm × 94 cm. Kenwood House, London, England. / Wikimedia Commons
p. 70	James Abbott McNeill Whistler, *Arrangement in grey and black No. 1*, 1871. Oil on canvas, 144.3 cm × 163 cm. Musée d'Orsay, Paris, France. / Wikimedia Commons
p. 72	Ludolf Bakhuysen, *Warships in a Heavy Storm*, c. 1695. Oil on canvas, 150 cm × 227 cm. Rijksmuseum, Amsterdam, the Netherlands. Purchased with support from the Rembrandt Association. / Wikimedia Commons
p. 74	Angelica Kauffmann, *Artist in the Character of Design, Listening to the Inspiration of Poetry*, 1782. Oil on canvas, 61 cm x 61 cm. Kenwood House, London, England. / Wikimedia Commons
p. 75	Sergiyn / Dreamstime
p. 76	Jacob van Ruisdael, *The Windmill at Wijk bij Duurstede*, c. 1668–1670. Oil on canvas, 83 cm × 101 cm. Rijksmuseum, Amsterdam, the Netherlands. On loan from the City of Amsterdam (A. van der Hoop Bequest). / Wikimedia Commons
p. 79	Franz Ludwig Catel, *Schinkel in Naples*, 1824. Oil on canvas, 62 cm × 49 cm. National Museums in Berlin, Nationalgalerie, Berlin, Germany. / Wikimedia Commons
p. 81t	Paolo Uccello, *The Battle of San Romano*, c. 1435–1440. Tempera on panel, 180 cm × 316 cm. Louvre Museum, Paris, France. / Wikimedia Commons
p. 81b	Painter of central Italy (formerly attributed to Luciano Laurana, c. 1420–1479), *View of an Ideal City, or The City of God*, c. 1470. Tempera on panel, 67.7 cm × 239.4 cm. Galleria Nazionale delle Marche, Urbino, Italy. / Wikimedia Commons
p. 83t	Carl Schweninger the Younger, *Gossip in the Salon*, c. 1903. Oil on panel, 47 cm × 60 cm. Private collection. / Wikimedia Commons
p. 83b	Georg Friedrich Kersting, *Embroidery woman*, 1817. Oil on panel, 47.5 cm × 36.6 cm. National Museum in Warsaw (MNW), Warsaw, Poland. / Wikimedia Commons
p. 84	Pierre-Auguste Renoir, *Luncheon of the Boating Party*, 1880–1881. Oil on canvas, 13 cm × 17.5 cm. The Phillips Collection, Washington, D.C., USA. Acquired 1923. / Wikimedia Commons
p. 85	Keystone Press / Alamy Stock Photo
p. 86	Barbara Hepworth, *Pelagos*, 1946. Part painted elm and strings on an oak base, 43 cm × 46 cm × 38.5 cm. Tate Gallery, London, England. Photo © Tate Museum, London, England.
p. 88	Vincent van Gogh, *Roses*, 1890. Oil on canvas, 71 cm × 90 cm. National Gallery of Art, Washington, D.C., USA. Gift of Pamela Harriman in memory of W. Averell Harriman. / Wikimedia Commons
p. 89	Vincent van Gogh, *Self-Portrait with Bandaged Ear*, 1889. Oil on canvas, 60.5 cm × 50 cm. The Courtauld Gallery London, England. / Wikimedia Commons
p. 91	Nicolas Poussin, *Self-portrait*, c. 1630. Red chalk on paper, 25.6 cm × 19.7 cm. British Museum, London, England. Art Heritage / Alamy Stock Photo
p. 92	Nicolas Poussin, *Winter or The Flood*, c. 1660–1664. Oil on canvas, 118 cm × 160 cm. Louvre Museum, Paris, France. / Wikimedia Commons
p. 94	Boris Kustodiev, *Boy with teddy bear*, 1907. Oil on canvas, 69.2 cm × 69 cm. State Tretyakov Gallery, Moscow, Russia. / Wiki Art
p. 95	Caspar David Friedrich, *The Sea of Ice or Polar Sea*, 1823–1824. Oil on canvas, 96.7 cm × 126.9 cm. Hamburger Kunsthalle, Hamburg, Germany. / Wikimedia Commons
p. 96	Richard Serra, *Fernando Pessoa*, 2007–2008. Weatherproof steel, 300 cm × 900 cm × 20.3 cm © Richard Serra / ARS, NY and DACS, London 2020. Photo: Joshua M. White. Courtesy Gagosian.
p. 98	Workshop of Andrea del Verrocchio, *Tobias and the Angel*, 1470–1475. Tempera on wood, 83.6 cm × 66 cm. National Gallery, London, England. / Wikimedia Commons

p. 101	Tim Ring / Alamy Stock Photo
p. 102	Helen Allingham, *A Cottage with Sunflowers at Peaslake*, c. 1848–1926. Watercolour, 20.3 cm × 24.1 cm. Private collection. The History Collection / Alamy Stock Photo
p. 103	Avalon / Photoshot License / Alamy Stock Photo
p. 104	Alexandre Zveiger / Shutterstock
p. 105	Raffaello Sanzio, *The School of Athens*, 1509–1511. Charcoal and white lead, 285 cm × 804 cm. Pinacoteca Ambrosiana, Milan, Spain. / Wikimedia Commons
p. 106	Giorgio Morandi, *Natura Morta*, 1953. Oil on canvas, 30.5 cm × 30.6 cm. © Photo by Antonia Reeve / Bridgeman Art Library. DACS 2020.
p. 107	Corepics VOF / Shutterstock
p. 108	Pieter Bruegel the Elder, *The Tower of Babel*, 1563. Oil on panel, 114.4 cm × 155.5 cm. Kunsthistorisches Museum, Wien, Austria. / Wikimedia Commons
p. 109	Caspar David Friedrich, *The Wanderer Above the Sea of Fog*, c.1817–1818. Oil on canvas, 98 cm × 74 cm. Hamburger Kunsthalle, Hamburg, Germany. / Wikimedia Commons
p. 110	Marcos Mesa Sam Wordley / Shutterstock
p. 111	Jacques-Louis David, *Napoleon Crossing the Alps or Bonaparte at the St Bernard Pass*, c. 1800–1801. Oil on canvas, 259 cm × 221 cm. Château de Malmaison, Rueil-Malmaison, France. / Wikimedia Commons
p. 112	Mateusz Delegacz / Unsplash
p. 113	Unknown sculptor, *Winged Victory* or *Nike of Samothrace*, c. 200–190 BCE. Parian marble, height: 244 cm. Louvre Museum, Paris, France. / Wikimedia Commons
p. 114(l)	Andre Tan / Unsplash
p. 114(r)	Pat Lauzon / Shutterstock
p. 115(l)	STIL / Unsplash
p. 115(r)	Shifaaz Shamoon / Unsplash
p. 116	Pieter de Hooch, *The Courtyard of a House in Delft*, 1658. Oil on canvas, 73 cm × 60 cm. National Gallery, London, England. / Wikimedia Commons
p. 117	Francisco de Zurbarán, *Still Life with Lemons, Oranges and a Rose*, 1633. Oil on canvas, 60 cm × 107 cm. Norton Simon Museum, Pasadena, USA. The Norton Simon Foundation. GL Archive / Alamy Stock Photo
p. 119	Christen Købke, *View of Østerbro from Dosseringen*, 1838. Oil on canvas, 39.5 cm × 50.5 cm. Kunst Museum, Winterthur, Switzerland. / Wikimedia Commons
p. 120	Gustave Caillebotte, *Young Man at His Window*, 1875. Oil on canvas, 117 cm × 82 cm. Private collection. / Wikimedia Commons
p. 121	Agnes Martin, *Stone*, 1964. Ink on paper, 27.7 cm × 27.7 cm. MoMA, New York, USA. © 2020 Estate of Agnes Martin / DACS 2020. Digital image: The Museum of Modern Art, New York/Scala, Florence.
p. 122	Bhuddist statue of Guanyin, Shanxi province, China, Jin dynasty, 1115–1234. Wood and pigments, 110.7 cm × 77.6 cm × 57.4 cm. National Gallery of Victoria, Melbourne, Australia. Felton Bequest, 1939. Photo: National Gallery of Victoria.
p. 124	Caspar Netscher, *The Lace Maker*, 1662. Oil on canvas, 33 cm × 27 cm. The Wallace Collection, London, England. / Wikimedia Commons
p. 125/126	Jacques-Louis David, *Belisarius Begging for Alms*, 1781. Oil on canvas, 312 cm × 288 cm. Palais des Beaux-Arts, Lille, France. / Wikimedia Commons
p. 130	Jonolist / Flickr (CC BY-SA 2.0)
p. 132	Jean Auguste Dominique Ingres, *Henry IV Receiving the Spanish Ambassador*, 1817. Oil on canvas, 39.5 cm x 50 cm. Petit Palais, Paris, France. / Wikimedia Commons
p. 133	Jacques Boulbene, *Henry IV, King of France and Navarre*, c. 1600. Oil on canvas. Musée des Augustins, Toulouse, France. / Wikimedia Commons
p. 136/138	Pottery decorated by members of the Bloomsbury Group © Estate of Duncan Grant. All rights reserved, DACS 2020.
p. 137	Photo © Tate Museum, London, England.
p. 140	Stickback Windsor Chair, 18th century. Photo: 1stDibs
p. 141	French Wing Back Chair, 19th century. Photo: 1stDibs

p. 142	Ludwig Mies van der Rohe, The Barcelona® Chair, 1929. Photo: Knoll
p. 143(t)	Andrey Elkin / Alamy Stock Photo
p. 143(m)	Igor Kovalchuk / Alamy Stock Photo
p. 143(b)	tarzhanova / 123RF
p. 145	Edvard Munch, *The Scream*, 1910. Tempera on panel, 83 cm × 66 cm. Munich Museum, Oslo, Norway. / Wikimedia Commons.
p. 146	Alma Thomas, *Elysian Fields*, 1973, acrylic on canvas, 76.5 × 107.2 cm. Smithsonian American Art Museum, Washington D.C., USA. / Bequest of the artist, 1980.36.8.
p. 147	Henri Rousseau, *Myself: Portrait-Landscape*, 1890. Oil on canvas, 146 cm × 113 cm. Prague National Gallery, Prague, Czech Republic. / Wikimedia Commons.

THE SCHOOL OF LIFE

The School of Life tries to teach you everything you need to have a good life that they forget to teach you at school. We have shops all around the world, we run a YouTube channel and we have written a lot of books specifically for younger people, including books about philosophy, art, architecture, nature and the best way to have a healthy and happy mind.

theschooloflife.com